TRACKS OF
THE CITY

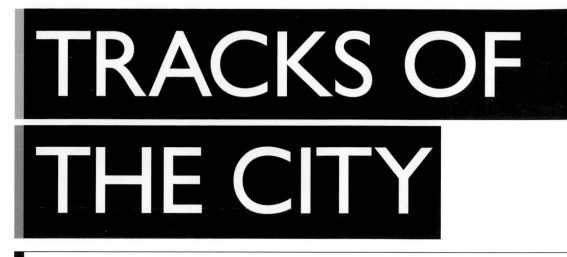

TRACKS OF THE CITY

An Introduction to the Railways,
Tramways and Metro in Dublin

DÓNAL MURRAY

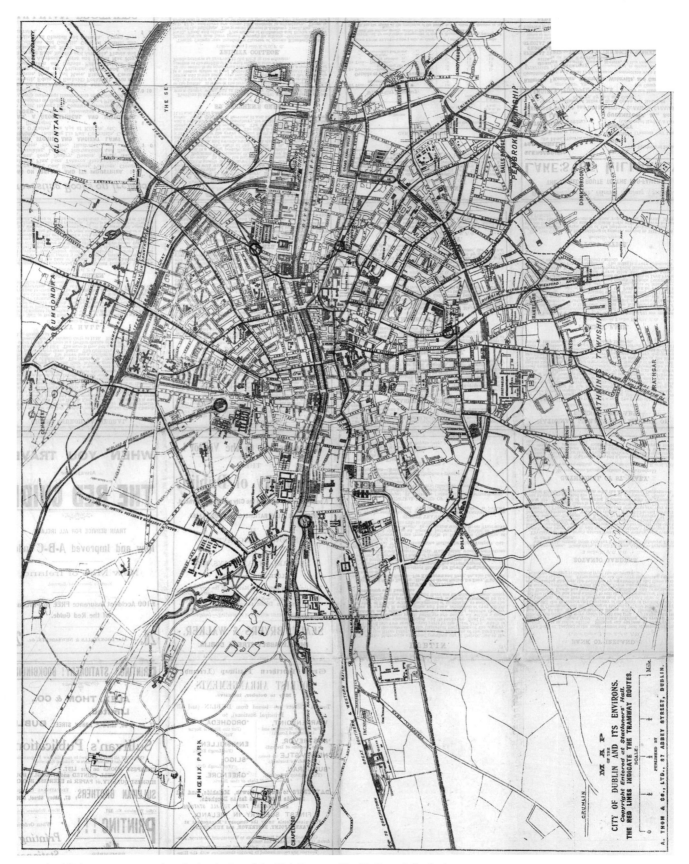

Map of Dublin's tramway network at the beginning of the 20th Century. *(Des McGlynn Collection)*

This book is dedicated to my father Denis Murray,
a professional railway man for thirty years. Quite a considerable portion
of his spare time was spent chasing or travelling on trains as a result of his
youngest son's interest in railways, so it must have felt at times that he never
had any time away from the day job. Never once did he complain, and a
better travelling companion one could not find.

Thank you Dad.

Published 2014 by Colourpoint Books
an imprint of Colourpoint Creative Ltd
Colourpoint House, Jubilee Business Park
21 Jubilee Road, Newtownards, BT23 4YH
Tel: 028 9182 6339
Fax: 028 9182 1900
E-mail: info@colourpoint.co.uk
Web: www.colourpoint.co.uk

First Edition
First Impression

A catalogue record for this book is available from the British Library.

Designed by April Sky Design, Newtownards
Tel: 028 9182 7195
Web: www.aprilsky.co.uk

Printed by W&G Baird Ltd, Antrim

ISBN 978-1-78073-057-8

Front cover: A new Mk 4 Intercity push-pull set awaits entry into service outside the Inchicore Works paint shop in September 2006.
(Dónal Murray)

Rear cover: (Top) Clontarf Road Dart Station appeared on the map over fifty years after the original Clontarf Station (located further
north on the former GNR main line) closed in 1956. The construction of the adjacent Eastpoint Business Park was a major factor in
creating the demand for a new station adjacent to the Fairview DART depot. *(Des McGlynn)*
(Below) Luas units on test at Mayor Street on the Red Line extension to The Point in 2009. *(Railway Procurement Agency)*

CONTENTS

PREFACE

This book is but a summary of the story of the railways, tramways and the planned metro in the capital city of the Republic of Ireland. It is the author's hope that this story will be of interest not only to transport enthusiasts, but also to the general reader with an interest in the workings of a metropolis, and how important it is to keep a capital city moving.

About the author

Dónal Murray was born in Dublin in 1970. He studied Quantity Surveying at the Dublin Institute of Technology and Construction Law and Administration (Post Graduate) at Trinity College. He has written several books about railways in both the Irish and English languages and has written three novels in Irish, in addition to several magazine and newspaper articles in both languages. He lives in Dublin with his wife and three children.

ACKNOWLEDGEMENTS

No book is possible without the contribution and assistance of a number of people. I would like to give sincere thanks to Malcolm Johnson and the team at Colourpoint, John and Jenny Smyth in Quebec, Barry Kenny, Joanne Bissett, Jane Cregan and Kevin Forde from Iarnród Éireann, Claire, Tom and Linda from the Railway Procurement Agency, Gordon Rowland from Dublin City Council, Simon Conry of the National Transport Authority, Sandra McDermott and Glenn Dunne at the National Photographic Archive, Paul Clerkin of archiseek.com, Claire Coulter of Wright Group, Josie McHugh of West Yorkshire PTE, Cyril McIntyre, Clifton Flewitt, Joe St Leger, Halton Borough Council, Cambridgeshire County Council, Jake Murray, Richie Murray, Denis Murray, Brian Kenny, Des McGlynn Snr & Des McGlynn Jnr.

I would also like to give my special thanks to my wife Paula and my children, Cillian, Sadhbh and Aoibhínn for their constant patience, support and love.

Dónal Murray
October 2013

The 'Enterprise' arriving at Amiens Street from Cork in the early 1950s behind GSR-built No 802 *Táilte*. From Amiens Street a GNR locomotive will take over for the Belfast (Great Victoria Street) leg of the journey. *(Seán Kennedy)*

CHAPTER 1

AN INTRODUCTION TO THE RAILWAYS, TRAMWAYS AND METRO IN DUBLIN

In 2014 Dublin will see the 180th anniversary of the departure of the first passenger train from Westland Row station (now Pearse Station) for Kingstown (Dún Laoghaire) on 17 December 1834. That year saw the start of a new kind of revolution in Ireland, unusually for the era, a non-violent revolution, and the commencement of great changes that would speed up life not only in the wealthier suburbs of Dublin, but throughout the country. Less than 90 years later, the island of Ireland would boast a rail network of some 3,442 miles with almost 19,000 employed by the railways. To understand the story of the rail lines of Dublin as they are today, we must look back at some of the political events and overall development of the railways and tramways that occurred on the island of Ireland during this period and in particular during the early part of the 20th century.

For the first two decades of the 20th century, there were five major passenger railway termini in Dublin, despite the fact that the city was a fraction of the size that it is in 2014. These termini belonged to some four companies. Railway services to the south-east of the city and beyond were in the hands of the Dublin and South Eastern Railway (DSER) with Ireland's first railway, the Dublin and Kingstown (D&KR), having been absorbed into the DSER by this time. Before 1907, the DSER had been called the Dublin, Wicklow and Wexford Railway (DWWR) and had originally been the Dublin and Wicklow Railway (DWR). In addition to the former D&KR terminus at Westland Row, the

Locomotive No 36 of the GSWR (Built 1847) with early carriages of the D&WR and D&KR in tow. There was no protection from the elements for the locomotive crew in the early days of the railways, and precious little for passengers in second or particularly third class either. This photo was taken at Inchicore Works in the 1930s. Thankfully these vehicles have been preserved, with the locomotive on a plinth inside Cork's Kent Station and the carriages in the Ulster Folk and Transport Museum at Cultra, County Down. *(GSR/Author's Collection)*

Top: Harcourt Street terminus, seen here in the early 1950s only had one passenger platform. To the right of the steam locomotives is a former Drumm Battery railcar set, either A or B, minus the batteries. These units were used for their last few years as hauled stock. *(Author's Collection)*

Centre: Harcourt Street station closed along with the inland route to Bray in 1958. The closure remained a topic of considerable controversy for decades afterwards. Although the terminus itself never reopened, most of the line eventually did in the form of the Luas Green Line. In 2004 Luas trams are seen on test in front of the former terminus building. *(Des McGlynn)*

Left: On the former D&KR section between Booterstown and Blackrock ex-DSER 4-4-2 tank locomotive No 455 of GSR class C2 is seen here heading south with a suburban working in the early 1950s. *(Seán Kennedy)*

DSER boasted another terminus, built by the Dublin and Wicklow Railway, at Harcourt Street. Suburban commuter services from these termini operated as far as Bray, and the DSER operated trains on lines to Rosslare, Waterford and Shillelagh.

In 1891 a line was built from the Westland Row terminus, over the streets of the capital and the River Liffey to the terminus of the Great Northern Railway (GNR) at Amiens Street. This line, built by the City of Dublin Junction Railway and known to this day as the 'loop line', provided an essential link between the two railways and also the Great Southern & Western Railway (GSWR) and Midland & Great Western Railway (MGWR), and would become a vital part of Dublin's commuter railways in the years to come. The GNR itself was formed in 1876, the result of various amalgamations including the Dublin and Drogheda Railway (DDR), the Ulster Railway (UR) and the Dublin and Belfast Junction Railway (DBJR).

To complete a direct line from Dublin to Belfast utilising the routes of the three different companies, the DDR, DBJR and UR, there was a major problem to overcome, an issue that resurfaced in the late 20th century regarding the Luas and the Metro in the capital, and that was the question of gauge. When

Ireland's first railway the D&KR was built, a gauge of 4 feet 8½ inches was used, as had been the case with the early railways in England. This gauge is generally known as standard gauge as it is a common standard used internationally. However railways were an emerging technology at that time, and the D&DR had their own idea about a suitable gauge and adopted 5 feet 2 inches for their line from Dublin to Drogheda. The Ulster Railway had different ideas again utilising a gauge of 6 feet 2 inches for their line from Belfast to Armagh. The government intervened through a Commission, initially declaring that the standard gauge for Ireland should be the same as the UR at 6 feet 2 inches. Eventually the Board of Trade declared that all the companies should compromise with a standard gauge of 5 feet 3 inches to be adopted as Irish standard gauge, the gauge that is still in use today for the main railway systems on the island of Ireland. The issue of gauge was to resurface again in the last few decades with arguments for and against the adoption of either 'international standard gauge' or the Irish standard gauge for new rail projects such as the Luas and Metro. In the end, the Irish standard gauge lost out for various reasons including the availability of 'off-the-shelf' rolling stock and the lack of integration of the new

Left: Westland Row Station, the original terminus of the Dublin and Kingstown Railway and known as Pearse Station since 1966. The building of the City of Dublin Junction Railway's line connecting the DSER with the GNR station at Amiens Street resulted in this station becoming a through station. *(Dónal Murray)*

Right: A brand new DART EMU on test in 1983 on the former City of Dublin Junction Railway's line between Tara Street and Pearse Station (formerly Westland Row). Trinity College is visible behind. Initially the College had reservations about the building of the line. *(Joe St Leger)*

lines with the existing main line or heavy rail network.

On the west side of Dublin city, the headquarters of the Great Southern and Western Railway (GSWR) was situated adjacent to the River Liffey at Kingsbridge. Having reached Carlow in 1846, by 1849 the GSWR main line had reached the north side of Cork city. Later the GSWR would extend to Waterford, Limerick, Tralee, Athlone and Sligo. Unlike either the DSER or GNR, the GSWR did not operate specific suburban commuter services, except for a very short period of time on its line from Islandbridge (at Kingsbridge)

around the north city loop, nor was there a requirement for the same on the largely undeveloped west side of the city at that time. The GSWR did however, possess extensive freight facilities at Kingsbridge and at North Wall in Dublin's Docklands.

To complete the picture of the termini and major railway companies in Dublin we go Broadstone, where the Midland and Great Western Railway had its terminus and works. The MGWR operated services to the principal destinations of Galway, Westport, Sligo and Cavan and various other locations served by its

Above: Opened in 1846, Heuston Station (formerly Kingsbridge) is the terminus for Intercity rail services to Waterford, Cork, Tralee and Limerick. From 1994 onwards it has also been the terminus of commuter rail services on the Kildare line. Ten years later in 2004, an interchange with the light rail Luas Red Line was provided and hopefully the future will see an underground station on the proposed DART Interconnector route provided. *(Iarnród Éireann)*

Right: Lucan South Station on the former GSWR main line in 1932. The station was approximately one mile distant from Lucan village and was never a particularly busy passenger station. It was closed to passengers in 1947. In this interesting photograph, one of the Drumm battery electric trains is on trial. These were quite revolutionary and it is sad to say that Lucan and the west Dublin suburbs are still awaiting the return of electrically powered trains! *(Author's collection)*

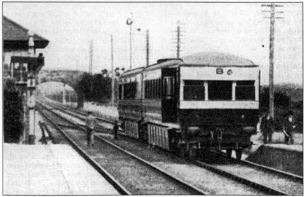

Top: Opened in 1847, Broadstone Station was the terminus for MGWR services to Galway, Sligo, Westport and Cavan until 1937, when passenger services were transferred by the GSR to Westland Row Station. The site retained its steam depot until 1961 whilst the bulk of the site passed to CIÉ provincial road services. Nowadays Broadstone serves as the headquarters and principal depot of Bus Éireann. Rails will once again return to part of the site with the arrival of the new Luas line from the city centre to Broombridge. *(Iarnród Éireann)*

Centre: Passenger services to Broadstone ceased in 1937. Here a service from Cavan behind exMGWR GSR class D6 No 544 is seen arriving at the former MGWR terminus in the early 1930s. *(Author's Collection)*

Right: Most Irish railway historians will probably be of the opinion that the last steam locomotive to be seen at Broadstone was in 1961. However, it was actually more than a decade and a half later, in 1975, when a small 0-4-0 steam locomotive built for another semi-state company, temporarily resided at the works, seen here with a young Des McGlynn Jnr. The locomotive in question was an Orenstein and Koppel locomotive built for the Comlucht Siúicre Éireann Teoranta (The Irish Sugar Company) and eventually it wound up preserved and in working order on Downpatrick and County Down heritage line. *(Des McGlynn)*

branch lines. One of the company's most important traffics was livestock. Like the GSWR, the areas it served to the immediate west of the city were sparsely populated and it did not operate specific suburban commuter services and, also like the GSWR, the MGWR had freight facilities at its Dublin terminus, and at North Wall. Cattle for the markets were handled at Liffey Junction.

The GSWR, MGWR, GNR and DSER were all eventually linked by the GSWR's line from Islandbridge under the Phoenix Park and the City of Dublin Junction Railway loop line. The primary reason for the construction of the GSWR's line from Islandbridge was not for passengers however, but to provide access to the Dublin docks for freight and livestock. All of these railway companies also possessed workshop

Above: Hauling a special train carrying a large number of passengers from a mass meeting of members of the Pioneer Association at Croke Park, a member of the 500 class emerges from the Phoenix Park tunnel at Islandbridge, heading south. In recent years there have been several suggestions both by politicians and in the media that there is no need for a DART interconnector tunnel due to the existence of this route. Although it does provide a cross-city link, it could not provide the connectivity that the interconnector could. *(Seán Kennedy)*

Left: One of Dublin's lesser known railway termini was actually owned by a large English railway company, the London and North Western Railway (LNWR). The station at North Wall, built with an adjoining hotel, only served for a short period of time as a railway terminus in the early 1900s. The LNWR did not operate any trains of its own into the station, but rail connections to the GSWR, MGWR and GNR were all possible via the network of lines at North Wall. The buildings later became the headquarters of CIÉ's and later, Iarnród Éireann's Civil Engineering Department. *(ArchiSeek)*

facilities in the capital with the exception of the GNR, whose works was located in Dundalk. One other major railway company, although not an Irish-based one, possessed a passenger railway terminus in Dublin at North Wall, that being the London and North Western Railway (LNWR). The LNWR did not operate any trains of its own, its terminus, adjacent to the LNWR hotel and steamer berth being served by GSWR trains for a period.

After the Irish War of Independence and the foundation of the Irish Free State in 1921, the new nation was on its economic knees and many of the traditional trade routes had been damaged by the partition of the island. The War of Independence was followed by the Civil War, and by the end of that turbulent and destructive period in 1923, the railways of the Free State were literally falling apart. The DSER in particular, had suffered extensive malicious damage and had lost a considerable portion of it rolling stock. There was a real threat that the railways might have to close, which was quite unthinkable as they were the only real transport and commercial arteries of the state at a time when road transport was still in its infancy. In 1924, the Free State government passed the Railways Act in the Dáil (Parliament) and the majority of the railways which lay completely within the boundaries of the state amalgamated into the Great

Southern Railway (GSR). It was early 1925 when the DSER joined the GSR (now Great Southern Railways). The GNR, being a cross-border concern, and some other minor railways that operated either wholly or partly in the Free State remained either independent or eventually closed down.

For the duration of its existence, the GSR struggled financially, and many different attempts were made to save money through the use of new technologies and reduction or even cessation of services on certain lines. In Dublin, the GSR built a number of railcar sets powered by batteries to the design of Dr James Drumm and these were used on commuter services on the DSER lines. In addition a number of localised colour-light signalling schemes were implemented, on the line south from Westland Row, at Kingsbridge and Harcourt Street, reducing the number of signal cabins needed and also the amount of maintenance required on the signalling system. The GSR's rationalisation programme also affected the Dublin area in a more negative fashion, with the former MGWR main line being singled west of Clonsilla and the Broadstone passenger terminus being closed. Passenger services on the former MGWR lines were then transferred to Westland Row station from 1937.

By the end of 'The Emergency', as the Second World War was known in Ireland, the GSR as a viable

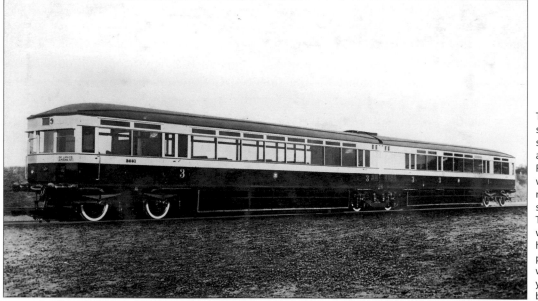

The GSR whilst cash-strapped, did try out some innovations such as the Drumm Battery Railcars. After initial trials with a converted Drewry railcar, four articulated sets eventually followed. The first two, A and B were to the design seen here in this official GSR photo. The latter two were built some seven years later to a different body design. *(GSR/IÉ)*

Whilst CIÉ was in the throes of modernisation, one last steam locomotive was produced at Inchicore, and a most unusual machine at that. CC1, colloquially known as 'The Turfburner', was built in 1957 to the design of OVS Bulleid. It never saw revenue earning service. *(CIÉ/Iarnród Éireann)*

company was just about out of steam, and again the government was forced to do something. As a result of the Transport Act 1944 a new company was created, Córas Iompair Éireann (CIÉ). CIÉ incorporated the tram and bus company the Dublin United Transport Company (Dublin United Tramways Company until 1941) and the GSR into one new organisation from 1945. The new company was a nominally private one with responsibility for almost all land-based transport in the city (with the exception of GNR road and rail services) and country, but the severe winters of 1946/47 put an end to any chance of the company's long term profitability. By 1950, the government was forced to act yet again with the nationalisation of CIÉ under yet another Transport Act. This time the Grand Canal Company was added into the mix but by this stage the last of the former DUTC tramways had closed, leaving the GNR's Hill of Howth Tramway as the only passenger tram line still functioning in the Republic of Ireland. Almost immediately,

the nationalised CIÉ put in place a programme of rationalisation and modernisation on the railways, the plan being to eliminate steam traction, CIÉ being one of the first European railways to do so. Ironically, modernisation of the CIÉ rail network may have started earlier, had it not been for a somewhat bizarre report by James Milne, formerly of the Great Western Railway in England. This report commissioned by the Department of Commerce, recommended retaining steam traction with limited experiments with diesel traction only, and also recommended retaining a considerable number of branch lines, on the basis that they fed into the core network.

By the end of the 1950s CIÉ was in the process of implementing a comprehensive plan to save money and achieve profitability, by the closure of hundreds of miles of the rail network around the country. In Dublin the MGWR's terminus at Broadstone had already been closed by the GSR with services diverted to Westland Row, but the news of the closure by CIÉ of

The former Navan line of the MGWR being lifted by a contractor near Dunboyne in the 1960s. *(Author's collection)*

Upon the dissolution of the GNR(B), CIÉ inherited half of the former's fleet of AEC and BUT railcars. A four-car AEC set is seen here at Amiens Street in the late 1960s. *(Des McGlynn)*

The GNR's BUT railcars were built at Dundalk Works, and were more powerful and flexible in terms of unit formation than the GNR's AECs. They were however incompatible with other stock. A six-car BUT set is seen here at Amiens Street signal cabin in the late 1960s. *(Des McGlynn)*

the Harcourt Street line was greeted with some shock, particularly as many of the suburbs along the line were in the process of expansion. The contemporary thinking was that buses were more than adequate to service the capital's commuting needs. By 1963, the former MGWR line from Clonsilla to Dunboyne and Navan had also closed completely and there were no passenger stations left open on the former MGWR route from Liffey Junction to Maynooth.

After years of struggle as a private cross-border entity, the GNR succumbed in 1953 to the control of a board jointly administered by the Stormont government in the North of Ireland and the Dáil in the Republic. This was only to last until 1958 when divergent policies regarding the railways in the two jurisdictions resulted in the dissolution of the GNR Board and the splitting of the remaining assets of the GNR. By this stage the cross-border routes of the GNR had all closed with the exception of the Dublin to Belfast line and the Portadown to Derry/Londonderry

route. In the Republic, the GNR's railway and stock were taken over by CIÉ, who wasted no time in closing the last remaining passenger tram line in County Dublin, the Hill of Howth tramway in 1959.

From the perspective of railway commuting, matters continued to deteriorate until the oil crisis of the early 1970s. There was complete lack of investment in the suburban rail services with clapped-out equipment becoming more common on the rails whilst the road fleet continued to modernise. Eventually there was a realisation that Dublin was becoming choked with road traffic. As a result CIÉ commissioned transport consultants AM Voorhees to do a study regarding the provision of a Rapid Transit system for the capital. Voorhees concluded that the motorway system planned for the capital at the time (and that has since been built) would eventually be unable to cope with the volumes of traffic predicted and that there would be a definite need for a rail rapid transit system by the 1980s!

CIÉ published a plan for a system of rapid rail lines

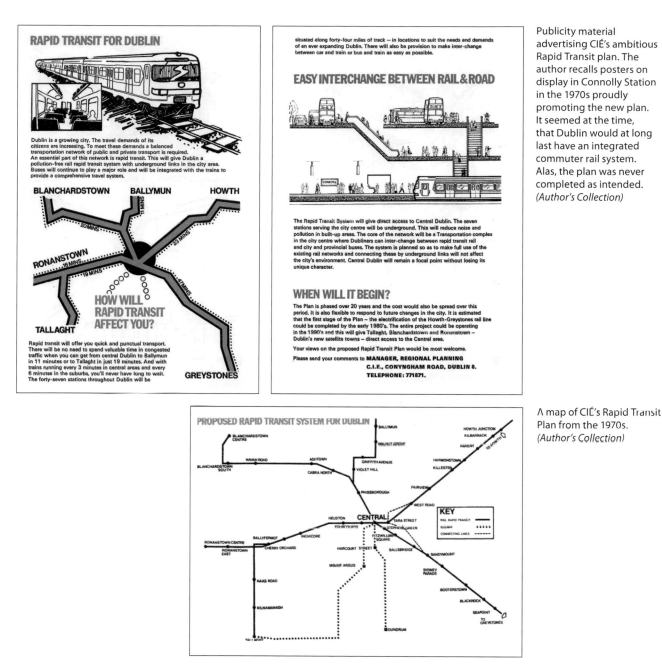

Publicity material advertising CIÉ's ambitious Rapid Transit plan. The author recalls posters on display in Connolly Station in the 1970s proudly promoting the new plan. It seemed at the time, that Dublin would at long last have an integrated commuter rail system. Alas, the plan was never completed as intended. *(Author's Collection)*

A map of CIÉ's Rapid Transit Plan from the 1970s. *(Author's Collection)*

radiating to Bray, Howth, Blanchardstown, Tallaght and Clondalkin/Lucan, with busways planned to Tallaght via Harold's Cross, and Dundrum. A rapid rail line to the Airport via Ballymun was also included together with a central bus and rail station in the city centre. Strangely enough, these lines covered many of the routes either built or included in the plans for the Luas and Metro. The most important difference of course being the comparative availability of land and cheaper prices at the time of the original plans, coupled with the fact that the whole development of the city may not have ended up road-based if the original plans had been implemented within the timeframe originally envisaged.

Alas, the government was not disposed to proceeding with CIÉ's plans, despite the obvious benefits, and of course it is now common knowledge that there were some serious issues with the general

The CIÉ Rapid Transit Plan included for two busway routes on the lines of the segregated but unguided system in Runcorn, Chesire, England. A bus is seen here near Runcorn's Shopping City on an elevated section of the busway shortly after its opening in the 1971. The busway is still in use today. *(Courtesy of Halton Borough Council)*

planning process in Dublin at that time. Had CIÉ's plan proceeded when originally intended, the system would have been completed by the mid 1980s, but nothing happened until the late 1970s/early 1980s, a period when the government seemed to change so often, it was difficult to keep track of who exactly was in power. At election time in 1979, one particular party declared that they would provide the funding for the electrification of the Howth to Bray commuter line (Phase 1 of the Rapid Transit plan). That particular party won that election, and despite an attempt to roll back on the promise, and the diversion of some European Community funding for the project to other areas, the DART line as we now know it was officially opened in summer 1984, and immediately impacted positively upon the public's perception of rail transport in the city.

During this politically turbulent period another politician facing election promised that the expanding suburban town of Maynooth would be provided with a

A new DART unit is shunted into Fairview Depot using an Inchicore designed and built special coupling bar in 1983. *(Des McGlynn)*

commuter rail service. With a total lack of any funding behind the promise, from 1981 CIÉ was forced into a position where it had to provide a commuter service with no additional resources. A number of intermediate stations reopened along the line in 1981, including Leixlip (Louisa Bridge), Clonsilla, and Ashtown. Lucan North was also originally intended to open but never did. It was another 13 years before new trains were provided for the Maynooth commuter service, but this time provided by Iarnród Éireann (a subsidiary of CIÉ from 1987). At the same time a commuter service had been instigated on the Kildare route from Heuston Station (Kingsbridge before 1966),

also serving Cherry Orchard, Clondalkin, Celbridge and Hazelhatch, and Sallins & Naas. The investments in commuter rail services to the west of the capital, whilst welcome, came quite late in the development phase of the western suburbs. Therefore they did not have quite the impact in creating a modal shift as they would have if they had occurred as originally envisaged many years before.

At around the same time, CIÉ's newly established Light Rail Project Office started planning for three light rail lines (later known as the Luas), radiating from the city to Dundrum, Tallaght and Ballymun. Unfortunately however, political interference once

Left: Leixlip was a quiet rural backwater on the former MGWR main line when this photo was taken in the 1950s. Today this location hosts the rebuilt Leixlip Louisa Bridge Station on the busy Maynooth commuter route. *(Seán Kennedy)*

Right: CIÉ commenced commuter services on the Maynooth line in 1981 on a shoestring budget with cascaded main line stock. The stations, such as Ashtown seen here, also remained basic well into the Iarnród Éireann era. *(Des McGlynn)*

Left: Lack of vision 1? Certainly! This is Harcourt Street in the 1920s with a tram of the DUTC heading south past Harcourt Street railway station, terminus of the DSER inland route from Bray. The tram lines were gone by the end of the 1940s and the railway line closed by the end of the 1950s. In 2004, the Luas Green Line was opened largely on the former railway alignment from Sandyford but descending to street level just before the old terminus, and following the route of the old tram lines down Harcourt Street to the new terminus at St Stephen's Green. *(Author's collection)*

Above: The same location as above in the current period with a Luas Tram. *(Jake Murray)*

again affected the plans, another change of government spelling the end for the Ballymun line and the city centre connection between the two remaining routes, delaying the project considerably and causing the loss of some European Union funding for the project. With the two planned light rail lines now separate entities and destined to be so for the best part of another two decades, two depots were now required instead of just one. At least, the authorities proceeded with the construction of what became the Luas Red Line (from Connolly Station to Tallaght) and the Green Line (from St Stephen's Green to Sandyford), the greater part of the latter being constructed on the formation of the old Harcourt Street line. These lines were opened in 2004 and, like the DART, from the very start were successful in attracting commuters from other modes of transport, proving once again that the provision of high quality rail-based commuter transport could even entice people out of their cars. Predictions by various vested interests, and some media commentators that the Luas would be a 'white elephant' were immediately discredited.

Lack of vision 2? In this photo, contractors are busy removing the railway bridge spanning the Grand Canal at Charlemont Bridge, a short distance south of the closed Harcourt Street terminus station. Less than 50 years later, the government spent a considerable sum of money reinstating a bridge in this very place, as part of the construction of the Luas Green Line. *(Leabharlann Náisiúnta na h-Éireann, O'Dea Collection)*

The same location as the previous photo from a different angle in 2003 with a new bridge in place. *(Dónal Murray)*

25

There was no doubt now that Dublin would benefit considerably from a comprehensive rail-based transport system, and with the creation of the Railway Procurement Agency and the Dublin Transport Authority, planning commenced in earnest for two Metro lines and more Luas lines. In addition Iarnród Éireann commenced work on its own plans for extensions to the DART, additional stations, the rebuilding of the line from Clonsilla to Dunboyne (later Navan), the multi-tracking of the Kildare route as far as Hazelhatch, and the all-important Interconnector, and other improvements to existing lines.

At the moment, the economic depression affecting the Republic of Ireland has affected a number of these plans and somewhat like CIÉ's plans of the 1970s, it is unclear as to when they might actually come to fruition. But extensive work has been carried out on the planning and design of Metro North, from Dublin's St Stephen's Green to Swords and Lissenhall via Dublin Airport. Metro West, an orbital route from Tallaght, skirting Lucan and Clondalkin and connecting with Iarnród Éireann at Fonthill and Porterstown and the planned Lucan Luas line, finally connecting with Metro North has also been substantially designed and has gone through some of the planning process. Several new Luas lines or extensions have also been planned, with some extensions already complete, such as the Red Line extensions to Citywest/Saggart and The Point at Dublin's Docklands, and the Green Line extension from Sandyford to Cherrywood. On Iarnród Éireann, the former MGWR Navan branch has reopened to beyond Dunboyne at Pace/M3 Parkway, although it is unclear when the planned Navan extension will go ahead.

Ireland's current economic state, and perhaps lack of vision on the part of some politicians has resulted in the stalling of many exciting developments planned for the capital's rail network, but one thing is certain, some amazing changes have taken place on the tracks of the city in the last 20 years after a generation of regression and contraction. Hopefully we will not have to wait for too long for economic recovery and some political vision and will to re-start the process of creating a fully integrated rail-based transport system for Dublin.

CHAPTER 2

IARNRÓD ÉIREANN LINES AROUND THE CITY

The 1970s did not exactly represent the heyday of railway investment in Dublin, although some limited progress was made with the commuter lines radiating north and south from Connolly Station. On the former GNR lines north of Connolly, new stations were opened at Bayside on the Howth branch and Kilbarrack. On the former DSER line to the south, a new station opened at Booterstown, adjacent to the marsh and wildlife preserve, which the original construction of the railway had helped to create. In addition to the new stations, some life-expired CIÉ AEC railcars were

converted into four and five-car push-pull commuter trains to operate with the re-engined former C(201) class locomotives. Regular Sunday services on the commuter lines, other than during the summer months, were still some years away however, as were services to the developing western suburbs.

At the end of the 1970s, road traffic congestion in the city was becoming a serious problem, and a period of political instability had commenced, with general elections becoming a frequent occurrence. Both of these factors would have an influence upon the rail

Bayside station on the Howth branch was opened by CIÉ IN 1972. At around the same time, and despite very limited resources, CIÉ rebuilt a number of de-engined railcar sets into push-pull sets to operate with 201 (Metro-Vick C) class locomotives. Unfortunately, the rebuilt sets were a case of 'cheap and nasty' and did nothing to encourage people out of their cars onto commuter trains. *(Joe St Leger)*

The last 'surviving' push-pull control car No 6111, a former AEC railcar, is seen here at Inchicore in 2005. Prior to the introduction of the DART services, the push-pull units in conjunction with the 201 class (former C class), just about maintained an acceptable suburban service on the Howth to Bray route. They were most unpopular with commuters though, and did nothing for the railway's image. *(Dónal Murray)*

Prior to the introduction of the 2nd generation DMUs in 1994, the Maynooth line and other outer suburban services did see some improvement in service quality with the introduction of push-pull Mk 3 sets and the 121 class locomotives as traction. *(Des McGlynn)*

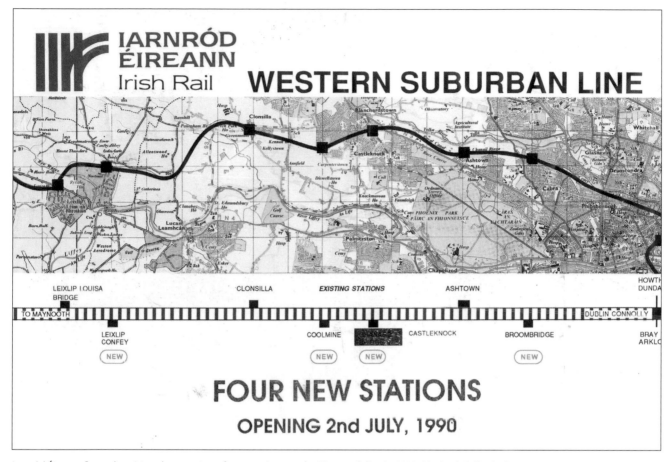

Iarnród Éireann flyer advertising the opening of new stations on the Maynooth line in 1990. *(Author's Collection)*

network. One particular political party announced that if elected to government again, they were willing to make substantial investment in public transport and particularly the commuter rail network, by giving CIÉ the go ahead with the first phase of its plan for Dublin. The plan in question was the first phase of the Dublin Rail Rapid Transit System, or what later became known as the DART (Dublin Area Rapid Transit). This first phase of the system involved the complete rebuilding and electrification of the Howth to Bray commuter lines. Not long after the construction of the DART had commenced, another election beckoned and another promise was made, this time that commuter rail services would be provided between Maynooth on the former MGWR line and Connolly Station, with stations at Drumcondra, Ashtown, Clonsilla, Lucan North and Leixlip (Louisa Bridge) by 1981. This promise was apparently made without consultation

with CIÉ nor with the provision of additional funding for the project or services.

Following a £113 million (Irish pounds) investment and an approximately five year lead-in period, the DART line, consisting of 34 km of double-track railway between Howth and Bray, opened in July 1984. The new service, with it's bright, comfortable and frequent electric multiple units providing a seven-days a week service, was an immediate hit with the commuting public. The Maynooth line's commuter service remained however the very poor cousin, with CIÉ forced to operate the infrequent service on a shoestring budget with clapped-out trains. Unsurprisingly, the line lacked capacity and was a frequent source of commuter complaints. In addition, the town of Lucan was denied any service at all, as the proposed station at Lucan North, never opened.

The Maynooth line had to wait until the early

1990s for any kind of worthwhile improvement. Back in the GSR days, the former MGWR main line to Galway had had one its double tracks lifted west of Clonsilla, with no passing loops until Maynooth. This created a physical barrier to the increase in commuter train frequency on the line, even if sufficient stock would have been available. Finally, funds were provided. In addition, several new suburban housing estates located near the Maynooth line were located some distance from the few stations provided, limiting the potential of the line for development. Finally, the need for further stations was also recognised and new stations were constructed at Broombridge, Castleknock, Coolmine and Leixlip (Confey). However, trains themselves were still scarce and unsuitable locomotive-hauled trains still struggled to cope with services. The year 1994 would however prove to be the start of some real positive change on the line.

With the realisation that Dublin's western suburbs were expanding at a rate so rapid that the road system would eventually cease to be able to cope with traffic volumes, something that had been highlighted in a report commissioned

Top: The Maynooth line eventually benefited from some completely new station buildings such as this one at Leixlip Louisa Bridge seen here in 2002. *(Dónal Murray)*

Centre: Clonsilla Station retains its manual signal cabin in 2014, although only to control the adjacent level crossing gates. *(Dónal Murray)*

Right: Before the arrival of the new railcars in 1994, commuters on the Maynooth line had to put up with a sparse service operated by an array of different cascaded rolling stock. The 141 class locomotive, two ex-BR Mk 2 carriages and a 'Dutch' generating van seen here in the 1990s did not represent the worst of such equipment, but such trains were not suited to suburban services, being slow to load and with a significant portion of the train being taken up with engines and generators, rather than seats! *(Des McGlynn)*

Above: LHB in Germany were the builders of the first DART units. From 1983 onward commissioning of the units and driver training commenced, with passenger services starting in 1984. The first unit 8101/8301 is seen here being unloaded at North Wall in 1983. *(Iarnród Éireann)*

Left: There was no comparison to be made between the DART trains and the push-pull units that preceded them. Immediately upon their introduction, commuters' perception of rail transport changed for the better. *(Iarnród Éireann)*

by CIÉ some twenty years earlier, commuter rail services were finally provided on the former GSWR line to Newbridge and Kildare in 1994. Stations were reopened at Clondalkin, Hazelhatch (for Celbridge), Sallins and a new station opened at Cherry Orchard. New diesel multiple units were acquired for these services, with additional units of the same type for the Maynooth line. The intention was to create, in effect, a 'diesel DART' and a new brand name was created for the Kildare route, 'Arrow'. The 'Arrow' brand name for this relatively infrequent low-density commuter service did not however quite make it into the common vocabulary of the commuting populace, nor indeed into common speech in quite the way the DART had, and the name eventually faded into distant memory.

The dawning of the new millennium finally heralded a series of serious investments in the Dublin commuter lines. The constrictions on the Maynooth line were finally eradicated with the opening of an extra line of rails between Clonsilla and Maynooth, and further new multiple unit sets enabled a far more frequent service, and indeed a Sunday service, to be provided on the

Top: The station that Fonthill replaced was the former GSWR Clondalkin station which had closed in the 1970s only to be re-opened in 1994 for the Arrow service, and then demolished when the line was multi-tracked. It is seen here in 2003 with 071 class, No 074 running towards Inchicore light engine. *(Dónal Murray)*

Centre: Hazelhatch station also reopened in 1994, serving the nearby town of Celbridge. By the early 2000s the 2600 class DMUs had largely been replaced on this service by the 2700 class. These units have since been withdrawn. *(Dónal Murray)*

Right: The 'Arrow' commuter service from Heuston to Kildare was launched in April 1994. There never had been a commuter service as such on this line before, although CIÉ's rapid transit plan from the early 1970s had proposed one. Notwithstanding the late start in the development of the service, investment has continued thankfully, with the line becoming multi-tracked as far as Hazelhatch by 2010. The future should eventually see the extension of DART services as far as Hazelhatch and beyond, via the Interconnector.
(Iarnród Éireann)

Maynooth line. New stations buildings were also provided, replacing the inadequate temporary structures that had been provided when the line and stations had first opened. Some of the station 'buildings' had in fact only been converted 20-foot containers. In 2008, an additional station was provided on the Maynooth line between Castleknock and Ashtown. Initially named 'Phoenix Park', the station has since been renamed 'Navan Road Parkway.' From 2007 onwards a service from Clonsilla to a new station at Docklands was also provided, operating via the former MGWR line to North Wall Docks. This provided a link from the Maynooth line to the redeveloped financial district of the city and would later form part of the service provided to Dunboyne and M3 Parkway on the reopened section of the former MGWR line to Navan.

On the line out of Heuston Station, huge investment was made in redeveloping the station itself (in excess of €11 million) and also as part of the Kildare Route Project, itself worth circa €350 million. New stations were constructed at Parkwest, Fonthill, Kishogue and Adamstown, together with a complete

Top: Most Maynooth services operate to and from Pearse Station although some terminate at Connolly. By the early 2000s most of these services were in the hands of the 2800 class DMUs, and later largely replaced by the 29000s. *(Dónal Murray)*

Centre: Clonsilla acquired a new station building similar to that built at Leixlip Confey in 2000, although as noted earlier, the ex-MGWR signal cabin remains in use in 2014 for the operation of the crossing gates. *(Dónal Murray)*

Left: A later addition on the Maynooth line was the brand new Phoenix Park station, later renamed Navan Road Parkway. *(Iarnród Éireann)*

rebuilding of Hazelhatch. Cherry Orchard station which had only ever been a temporary structure, under-used and heavily vandalised, was closed, as was Clondalkin (replaced by Fonthill). The new station at Kishogue, built to serve a proposed housing development, has not opened at the time of writing, but may do so in 2014. In addition to the new stations, two additional tracks were laid alongside the original GSWR main line to allow for the separation of commuter and inter-city trains and a greater frequency of services, allowing a capacity increase from 11,000 commuters a day to 36,400 by early 2010.

Top: There are eight platforms in use at Heuston at present, although curiously, there is a Platform 10 also! Whilst Heuston was being refurbished and expanded in 2003, Platform 10, a temporary platform adjacent to the line to the Phoenix Park tunnel, was provided for Kildare line commuter trains. *(Dónal Murray)*

Centre: The new station at Fonthill/Clondalkin opened on 13 October 2008 and replaced the former GSWR-built Clondalkin Station. This new station was built to facilitate an interchange with the planned Metro West line and boasts a substantial car park which, probably due to the stalled development of the immediate surrounding area, is usually quite empty at present. *(Dónal Murray)*

Above: Quite a number of stations have been opened on the lines around Dublin over the past few years. In this photo, a passenger purchases the first ticket sold at the just-opened Adamstown Station, Lucan on 10 April 2007. The South Lucan area had waited some 60 years for a passenger to be able to purchase a ticket in a local station. *(Dónal Murray)*

Right: The first regular passenger train to serve Adamstown, a Newbridge service seen here, called at 06:50 on the 10 April 2007. This was the first time in some sixty years that the Lucan area had a passenger train service on this line. *(Dónal Murray)*

The new millennium also witnessed an expansion of DART services to Greystones and Malahide, and the opening of new stations on the DART line at Clontarf Road and Grand Canal Dock, both of which serve nearby commercial developments. The DART fleet itself also doubled in this period. It is an interesting point of note that the DART station at Tara Street, in Dublin city centre is the busiest station on the entire rail network. By the end of the first decade of the new millennium, more than 90,000 people were using the DART, a substantial increase from the approximately 35,000 people using the service in 1984. Iarnród Éireann spent more than €75 million on the mentioned improvements in the early 2000s, but to further improve frequency, the signalling system in the city centre area requires significant upgrading to allow up to 20 trains per hour between Connolly and Pearse Stations. At present only 12 trains per hour

Connolly Station from the air: Until 1966, this important former Great Northern Railway terminus station was known as 'Amiens Street'. In the centre of the photograph the 'Loop Line' that connects the former DSER lines to the south with the lines to Maynooth/Sligo and the lines to Howth and the north may be seen. This line forms part of the DART's route as well as handling Intercity services to Rosslare and outer commuter services, but it is also the bottleneck that is restricting the increase in frequency of DART services. Only 12 trains per hour can use this section, and to improve frequency a new signalling system is required and ultimately the by-passing of the route by some services via the future Interconnector.

On the right hand side of the photo, the former GNR terminus may be seen, nowadays the terminus for services from Sligo and Belfast. The photograph was taken in the 1980s before substantial redevelopment of the surrounding area. *(Iarnród Éireann)*

can be permitted on this section, which restricts any improvement to the service.

In a way, the DART has been somewhat of a victim of its own success. Like many major railway and public transport projects, there were a number of politicians, media commentators and members of the public who doubted whether investment in the DART would be worthwhile, but the growth in passenger numbers conclusively proves beyond a shadow of a doubt that, not only was the investment worthwhile, but an absolute necessity. That said, further investment is still required to realise the true capacity of the DART, and the city centre resignalling and indeed the Interconnector, are vital elements required to this end.

Above: Maybach-engined No E432 shunts main line stock at Connolly station in the early 1970s. *(Des McGlynn)*

Left: Howth Junction was a busy place on this day in September 1979 with special trains being run to the temporarily re-opened Ashtown station conveying passengers to the Phoenix Park to attend a mass held by Pope John Paul II. *(Joe St Leger)*

Top: June 1984 heralded a new beginning for Howth line commuters with the arrival of the DART. *(Joe St Leger)*

Centre: The sidings at Malahide Quarry were frequently used to store old stock up until the removal of the sidings in the 1980s. In this 1970s view a B201 class hauls a southbound outer suburban train consisting of a four-wheeled heating van and a mixture of Park Royal and CIÉ-built carriages. *(Des McGlynn)*

Right: Liner trains were a common sight on the former GNR line in the 1970s, but not so common was the sight of two A/001 class at the head of a liner train, seen here heading for the capital at Malahide Station. *(Des McGlynn)*

Above: The DART extension to Malahide had yet to open when this photo was taken. Driver training and testing was still ongoing. A nearly new six-car 2700 class DMU stands alongside one of the original DART series units. *(Iarnród Éireann)*

Left: The DART was finally extended to Malahide from Howth Junction early in the new millennium, but Malahide continued to be served by DMUs of a number of types on outer commuter services, such as the 2900 class built by CAF in Spain. These unit are perhaps the most comfortable commuter trains introduced to date. *(Dónal Murray)*

In the early years of this century, substantial investment has been made in the DART. In this photo, one of the 8500 series units constructed in Japan is being offloaded at North Wall Docks, Dublin. *(Iarnród Éireann)*

Left: In addition to handling commuter and DART services, Intercity services to and from Rosslare, Sligo and Belfast use Connolly Station. These days the bulk of Intercity services use diesel multiple units, but until the mid 2000s, the 071 class locomotives were in charge of Rosslare and Sligo services, hauling Mk 2 air conditioned stock. The 071 class locomotives remain in service on freight and permanent way work. *(Dónal Murray)*

By the mid-1980s services between Howth and Bray were in the hands of the DART electric multiple units. However CIÉ, later Iarnród Éireann, badly needed new diesel powered trains for outer commuter services, but resources were scarce. As the production of Intercity Mk 3 carriages at Inchicore Works was nearing an end, it was decided to build five Mk 3-based push-pull sets to work with 121 class locomotives. These carriages were destined to be the last new-build carriages constructed in the Works. Until superseded from the mid-1990s onwards by new DMUs, these trains operated outer commuter services to Dundalk and Arklow, latterly using GM 201 class locomotives as motive power and later still, being transferred to secondary Intercity services. One of the new trains is seen here on test at Dundalk in 1988. *(Iarnród Éireann)*

Top: The first sign that things were about to improve for rail commuters on the non-electrified suburban lines was the announcement that 17 new railcars would arrive in 1994. The artist's impression presented a very Japanese looking DMU, quite different from the final appearance of what was to become the 2600 class. *(Iarnród Éireann)*

Centre: Commuters on other non-electrified routes such as the Maynooth line had to wait until at least 1994 before the arrival of any trains coming close to the standard of the DART units. Iarnród Éireann used units constructed by Mitsui in Japan, the first trains built in Asia for an Irish railway, to commence commuter services on the Kildare route in addition to improving the standard of service on the Maynooth line. The first unit is seen here in Japan. Note the dual gauge tracks and Japanese overhead line equipment. *(Iarnród Éireann)*

Right: Branded as the 'Arrow' for the new Kildare route service, the 2600's were also utilised on Maynooth and Northern outer suburban services. It was intended that the diesel units would provide a standard of comfort close to that of the DART. As can be seen from this interior view, the layout was quite spartan and the seats were actually quite hard, but there was no doubt that the new units were a vast improvement for commuters. *(Iarnród Éireann)*

Top: A few years later another batch of DMUs arrived to a broadly similar specification, although this time built in Spain. The 2700 class, an example seen here at Clontarf Road when new, took over or shared a number of routes with the 2600s before eventually ending up based in Limerick. These units were not quite as successful and although newer than the 2600s, it is the 2700 class that has been the first second generation DMU class to be withdrawn from service. *(Iarnród Éireann)*

Centre: Perhaps the most successful of the first three batches of new DMU's has been the 2800 class. Built by the same manufacturer in Japan as the 2600s, the 2800s certainly have higher quality seating than their Japanese predecessors. The first 2800s are being unloaded at North Wall from the ship's hold after their long voyage in this dramatic photograph. *(Iarnród Éireann)*

Right: A new Intercity Railcar (ICR) 3-car set rounds Bray head under the DART wires on a Rosslare service. These sets have displaced the 071 class and Mk 2 air conditioned carriages, and indeed the commuter railcars that served in the iterim on Intercity services from Connolly Station. These 22000 class units also operate outer-suburban commuter services from Heuston to Kildare, Portaoise, Carlow and Athlone, in addition to other Intercity services. *(Iarnród Eireann)*

ICR sets, built by Rotem in Korea now handle most Intercity and outer suburban commuter services out of Heuston Station. Cork-bound Intercity services remain loco-hauled/propelled using Mk 4 push-pull sets and EMD 201 class locomotives. (Iarnród Éireann)

What is now known as Pearse Station was in fact the first railway terminus in the city. Opened in 1834 as Westland Row, it was initially the terminus of the Dublin and Kingstown Railway and later became a through station. From 1937 to 1973, Pearse station also acted as the terminal station for rail services on the former MGWR route to Galway, Sligo and Westport, but nowadays only serves as a commuter/Dart station. *(Dónal Murray)*

The old order of re-engined C class locomotives and cascaded main line stock seen here at a pre-DART Dún Laoghaire in 1981. Whilst such trains kept the commuters moving, they projected a poor image. The arrival of the DART changed the travelling public's perception of rail commuting completely. *(Richie Murray)*

Top: The former DSER line to the south passes underneath one of the stands at Landsdowne Road (now known as Aviva Stadium), and when rugby, soccer or concerts are being played there, the station and its environs can become incredibly busy. This photo was taken in the early 1970s, long before the line was electrified for the DART and a generation before the total reconstruction of the stadium. AEC engined railcar No 2659 heads towards Wicklow (Murrough) Station with a commuter train. *(Joe St Leger)*

Centre: Just beyond Landsdowne Road station to the south, a short branch once diverged serving the Royal Dublin Society (RDS) at Ballsbridge. The line became particularly busy with horse traffic at the time of the Spring Show. The line was finally closed in the 1970s and the site of the branch terminus had been obliterated and is now occupied by a bank. Metrovick C (201) Class No 211 is seen here in the short-lived black and white with yellow front panel livery used in the 1960s, hauling a string of cattle wagons. *(Des McGlynn)*

Left: Although the RDS branch at Ballsbridge had closed in the 1970s, the year 1981 saw another rail vehicle arrive at the RDS for a show. This time it arrived on a low loader and was a product of British Rail Engineering and Leyland Bus. Northern Ireland Railways (NIR) management were so impressed, they bought it. It later served on the Portrush branch and is now preserved at Downpatrick. *(Des McGlynn)*

Left: One of the worst rail accidents to occur on the Dublin commuter rail network happened at Dalkey in 1979 when two passenger trains collided as a result of faulty signals. There were no fatalities, but there were a number of serious injuries, including the driver of one of the trains, a neighbour of the author. In this 1950s view a relatively new A class in original silver livery is seen at the station. *(Iarnród Éireann)*

Heading south from Dalkey station the line enters a short tunnel at the site of the 1979 accident. Upon emerging from the tunnel a beautiful view unfolds across Killiney Bay. In this photo one of the 8500 class DART units is seen rounding the bay. These units were designed with air-conditioning to enable them to be used in a future Interconnector tunnel. *(Iarnród Éireann)*

Above: Killiney Bay again but looking towards Dublin in the pre-DART days of the 1970s. A pair of 121 class led by 128, head south for Rosslare. Pairs of 121s or multiples of 121s, 141 and 181 classes were the usual motive power for such trains in the 1970s and 1980s. *(Seán Kennedy)*

Right: This view from a bridge on Sheriff Street in the early 1970s has vanished forever. Over the past 20 years or so, Iarnród Éireann's freight activities have considerably shrunk. The new Docklands Station now occupies this site, used by services to Clonsilla and Dunboyne and the M3 Parkway. The intention is to extend these services eventually to Navan and also to construct an underground DART station at this location. *(Des McGlynn)*

Above: This view from the same bridge on Sheriff Street in 2003 has also vanished forever. After the closure of the North Wall container yard on the far side of the bridge, a temporary facility occupied this site for less than a decade until it was redeveloped as the Docklands Station. *(Dónal Murray)*

Left: Over the other side of the bridge, extensive yards were still in place in 2001, with the tracks in the foreground leading to the former Bell Lines yard and the former LNWR terminus. This scene was swept away by the Spencer Dock Development. *(Dónal Murray)*

Top: The new Docklands Station opened in 2007, initially with a service to and from Clonsilla on the Maynooth line, and utilising the former MGWR route to North Wall. *(Iarnród Éireann)*

Right: Docklands Station was used for a combined Iarnród Éireann and emergency services exercise in July 2012, when a mock collision between a train and car was staged. There were no real casualties! *(Iarnród Éireann)*

Above: A tramway runs down the length of Alexandra Road in Dublin Port and actually belongs to the Dublin Port Company. There were once many rail connected sites along the tramway. A major one that is still in use is used for Tara mines ore trains. In the last few years container freight or liner trains have once again returned to the tramway.
(Des McGlynn)

Centre: In the 1970s this tiny BP-owned Planet shunter was still at work in the Port shunting fuel tankers. Its duties were later taken over by road tractors. *(Des McGlynn)*

Left: Rail-borne container freight is making somewhat of a comeback in Dublin Port. Formerly the bulk of container freight was handled in Iarnród Eireann's North Wall yard, adjacent to the former LNWR terminus. This yard vanished under development in the early 2000s. A common user terminal on Dublin Port land off Alexandra Road now handles rail container freight. *(Iarnród Éireann)*

CHAPTER 3
RAILWAY WORKS AND DEPOTS

To maintain the railway fleet and help keep the city moving, Iarnród Éireann has a number of facilities. The largest is of course Inchicore Railway Works, situated 1¾ miles from Heuston Station on the Cork main line. 'The Works', as it is known, opened in 1846 and was one of the largest industrial complexes in the state for a considerable period. In addition to maintaining locomotives and rolling stock, The Works produced locomotives until the early 1960s and carriages until the 1980s. At one time it employed more than 2000 people and often employed several generations of families. All sorts of trades people were

Opened in 1846, Inchicore Works occupies some 73 acres. At one time it was one of the largest industrial complexes in the country and produced and maintained almost everything that a railway could need. During the First World War, War of Independence and Second World War (or 'The Emergency' as the latter was known in neutral Éire) 'The Works' produced some munitions and armoured vehicles. In the periods of GSR and CIÉ control up until the 1970s, The Works also produced buses for both the Dublin and provincial fleets. *(Iarnród Éireann)*

Two of the more unusual locomotives to be assembled inside the Erecting Shop (later Diesel No 1) in the mid 1950s were these Walker Brothers locomotives, two of a trio of the F501 class, for the narrow gauge West Clare section. *(Seán Kennedy)*

The last main line locomotives to be built at Inchicore were Nos 1100 and 1101, later B113 and B114. Built with Sulzer engines in 1950/51, these locomotives soldiered on until the early 1970s. After spending several years in the Inchicore 'sound barrier', B114 was scrapped but thankfully B113 was preserved and cosmetically restored for the 1996 Inchicore Works open day. It is now in the care of the Railway Preservation Society of Ireland. *(Dónal Murray)*

employed there and it also boasted its own Medical Centre, Fire Service and 'Police' service at one time.

In the last few years the importance of The Works has declined somewhat. With the arrival of the first generation of commuter diesel multiple units in the 1990s a new maintenance depot opened in Drogheda specifically for the day-to-day maintenance of the commuter fleet. However, heavy repairs continued to be carried out at Inchicore. Likewise, the DART fleet, from its inception in 1984, had a maintenance depot of its own at Fairview, with Inchicore undertaking occasional heavy duty repairs. With the arrival of Intercity multiple units in the

B114 was the second of the original main line diesels. Originally numbered 1101, B114 lasted in service until 1974. Like its sister locomotive it spent some time in the Inchicore sound barrier but eventually it was cut up for scrap. One of the later B101 class Sulzer-engined locomotives is seen behind B114 at Inchicore Works. The B101 class were built by BRCW and the 12 engines used had originally been purchased for 6 twin engined locomotives that were intended to built at Inchicore Works before the Milne Report put paid to that plan. *(Des McGlynn)*

A class of five shunting locomotives preceded the Nos 1100 and 1101. In 1947 No 1000 emerged from Inchicore Works. Built in the Erecting Shop using Brush Electrical equipment and Mirelees engines, these locomotives were later renumbered into the D301 class and lasted until the early 1970s. No D302 is seen here in the company of a C class on the left and an Inchicore-built E401 class on the right. (Des McGlynn)

last few years, further maintenance work has been transferred to a new facility in Portlaoise.

The Fairview DART depot has quite an interesting history, commencing life as Ireland's first purpose built diesel multiple unit maintenance depot in the 1950s. Built by the GNR, the facility maintained the GNR's pioneering fleet of AEC railcars. When CIÉ took over the GNR lines in the Republic in 1958, it served as a CIÉ railcar depot, and later the depot for the CIÉ push-pull commuter trains. It was then totally rebuilt for the arrival of the DART fleet in the early 1980s. In 2001 a disastrous fire occurred, which all but destroyed the depot and completely destroyed a DART unit, but the depot managed to soldier on, maintaining the DART fleet seven days a week, and has since been reconstructed.

Right: Inside 'Diesel No 1' or 'The Motive Power Shop' as it is now known and once known as 'The Erecting Shop', This is the site where locomotive building finally concluded in the 1960s. It was also the workplace of the author's father, Denis Murray, for some 30 years. *(Dónal Murray)*

Below: Another view inside 'Diesel No 1'. A fantastic cut-away diagram of an A Class locomotive adorns one gable, although it was damaged at some stage and no longer lights up for demonstration purposes. *(Dónal Murray)*

In addition to routine repairs and maintenance, Inchicore works has had cause to carry out some very heavy repairs and rebuilding over the years. During the Northern Ireland conflict, a number of CIÉ trains were hijacked north of the border, the crews removed and locomotives and rolling stock wrecked. Inchicore Works had a number of personnel who made a sort of specialisation out of rebuilding all-but destroyed locomotives, one of which was the author's father, Denis Murray, who is seen here (sixth from left) with the crew responsible for rebuilding No 146 in 1978. *(Iarnród Éireann)*

Being an extensive industrial facility, Inchicore Works has its own team of firefighters. In this photo a fire fighting demonstration takes place. *(Iarnród Éireann)*

Inside Diesel No 1 at Inchicore, No 131 is stripped down for maintenance in September 2002. A 071 class is in similar condition behind it. The 121 class were the first really reliable diesel locomotives on the CIÉ system when introduced in 1961. Their only drawback was the single cab and thought was given to adding a second cab at Inchicore, but it never happened. *(Dónal Murray)*

Inchicore's carriage shed burned down in the 1990s and was subsequently rebuilt with a new roof, earning it the nickname 'Gare du Nord'. *(Dónal Murray)*

Inchicore Works in 1994. Six of the brand new EMD-built 201 class locomotives are lined up
for an official photograph. A new phase of modernisation has begun! (Iarnród Éireann)

In the summer of 1996, the Carriage Shop played host to an unusual collection of stock. Prior to the Inchicore Works open day of that year,
preserved ex-GSWR 0-6-0t No 90 and CIÉ-built Maybach diesel No E428, both of which had operated with the preservation group Westrail, were
given a make-over. No 90 had spent many years on a plinth at Mallow station before being loaned to Westrail along with E428 for heritage use on
the Athenry to Tuam line. The heritage operation eventually folded however. Also visible in this photo is a new De Dietrich Enterprise carriage in
the left background, and the BREL earlier in the right background, the latter still being in its BREL livery at this point. (Dónal Murray)

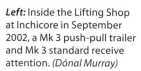

Left: Inside the Lifting Shop at Inchicore in September 2002, a Mk 3 push-pull trailer and Mk 3 standard receive attention. *(Dónal Murray)*

Below: Although there is a diesel multiple unit maintenance facility at Drogheda, Inchicore still carries out certain maintenance and heavy repairs to the commuter fleet. *(Dónal Murray)*

A new Mk 4 intercity push-pull set rests outside the Inchicore Works paint shop where a Spanish-built DART unit is receiving attention in 2006. *(Dónal Murray)*

In 2006 Inchicore's running shed could still boast a variety of 'baby GM' types including the 141 and 181 classes. All of these locomotives have since been withdrawn. *(Dónal Murray)*

Above: Inchicore's Diesel No 2 shop also known as 'The Ramps' was never quite as busy looking as Diesel No 1, the former Erecting Shop and now the Motive Power Shop. Here a 201 class locomotive, still in original livery receives attention in 2006. *(Dónal Murray)*

Left: Outside of Diesel No 1/Motive Power Shop on a sunny afternoon in 2006, 201 class No 218 is seen having been recently repainted into the new intercity livery. Alongside is another 201 class in original and slightly scruffier livery. *(Dónal Murray)*

Right: End of the line for the first real successful CIÉ main line diesel locomotives. Introduced in 1961, EMD's GL8 type, known in Ireland as the 121 class gave four decades of solid service before ending up in the scrap line at Inchicore. *(Dónal Murray)*

Below: 2750 class 'bubble car' bi-cab unit required major body repairs after a crash near Limerick in the mid 2000s. It is seen here in Inchicore in 2006. *(Dónal Murray)*

Top: The BREL-designed air conditioned Mk 2 carriages served CIÉ/IÉ well for four decades. In 2000, a number were completely refurbished at Inchicore and given a special livery for Galway line services.
(Dónal Murray)

Centre: During 1990 a number of ex-British Rail Mk 2 carriages were purchased from a scrap merchant and rebuilt at Inchicore. Two of these non-air conditioned carriages are seen here being rebuilt in that year.
(Des McGlynn)

Left: Inside the Carriage Shop at Inchicore in summer 1996. This is the part-completed, but never finished, driving trailer for the former BREL set of carriages. This former BREL BSO, part of a demonstration set, never did have its driving cab fitted and the former BREL International carriages never operated as a push-pull set as had been intended.
(Dónal Murray)

Top: The interior of the Plant Shop at Barrow Street. This was originally a DSER loco shed opposite the former Grand Canal Street Works. The Plant Department was relocated to Kildare when a new station, Grand Canal Dock, was opened at this location in 2001. *(Richie Murray)*

Fairview is the site of the DART maintenance depot. Although severely damaged in a fire in 2001, the depot carried on functioning and has since been fully repaired. *(Iarnród Éireann)*

The original LHB-built DART units were completely refurbished in the early 2000s by Siemens and re-commissioned back into service at the rebuilt Fairview Depot. *(Iarnród Éireann)*

Above: Iarnród Éireann's commuter diesel multiple unit fleet is maintained at a dedicated depot in Drogheda, opened in 2003 at the site of the original Dublin and Drogheda Railway terminus. *(Iarnród Éireann)*

Left: Inside the Heuston Valeting Plant in January 2002 a Mk 3 push-pull trailer receives a cleaning. This plant is now used for ICR maintenance. *(Dónal Murray)*

CHAPTER 4
TRAMWAYS

In 1829 the first omnibus service was founded in London. Some six years later it was announced that Dublin would have a bus network. However, there were some vested interests opposed to this idea and changes to the laws were necessary to permit such a service. The Police Act of 1848 provided the legal foundation for the first (legal) bus service to begin in Dublin. At this time the population of Dublin was a little more than a quarter of a million souls, and the city lay generally within the confines of the two canals, but was gradually stretching out southwards towards Rathmmines and Rathgar. These new suburbs badly needed some form of public transport and the introduction of a horse-drawn bus service was most welcome. It didn't take too much longer for the horse-drawn bus network to spread to other areas.

Trams from Terenure (No 15) and either Dalkey (No 8) or Dún Laoghaire (No 7) approach the statue of Daniel O'Connell on the capital's main street. In the distance is Nelson's Pillar where the trams will terminate. *(Railway Procurement Agency)*

The majority of the city's tram lines converged at Nelson's Pillar in O'Connell Street. The trams and the Pillar have long since disappeared, although trams in a new guise are destined to return. In this view a number of trams are visible along with the odd bus but little other traffic. *(Author's Collection)*

In 1832, a further development occurred in New York that would revolutionise urban public transport when an Irishman by the name of John Stephenson built a horse-drawn carriage to go on rails. It was much easier for a horse to pull a loaded carriage on smooth rails rather than on rough roads and of course it was far more comfortable for the passengers. By 1859, the horse tram had reached Europe and new laws were enacted in Ireland, the Tramways Acts 1869 and 1876, to facilitate and regulate such developments. Regulation was required as it was recognised quite early on that there was a need to protect existing services that used the roads already, for example gas, sewerage and water mains, etc. The tramways were also subject to inspection by the Railways Inspecting Officer before they could be opened to the public, just like the railways. Normally, the inspecting officer would be a former British Army officer (Royal Engineers).

The Dublin City Tramway Company was the first tramway to receive permission to build. The DCTC's plan was to build a tramway between Kingsbridge and Harcourt Street via Westland Row, thereby connecting all of the major railway stations south of the River Liffey. However the plan ultimately failed and the first tram line to actually open in the city was that of the Dublin Tramway Company between College Green and Rathmines, on 1 February 1872. The line was built to the same gauge as the railways 5 foot and 3 inches (1600 mm), and would later extend northwards to Nelson's Column and southwards to Terenure. Ironically, one of the last traditional tram lines to close in Dublin in the 1940s, was the line to Terenure. On the first day of public travel over the line, 2,055 passengers used the service.

At an industrial exhibition in Berlin in 1879, Werner Von Siemens' electrically powered locomotive made its debut. It only took another four years before this revolutionary new form of traction made its appearance on a public tramway, with the opening of the Giant's Causeway line in County Antrim. Two years later and another electric tramway opened in Ulster, the Bessbrook and Newry Tramway. It wasn't long before the Dublin tramway operators looked at phasing out the horse in favour of electric traction. By the 1890s a number of Dublin's tram companies had amalgamated and a company by the name of the Dublin United Tramway Company (DUTC) announced its intention to abandon horse traction altogether. Like most public transport developments there were those both sceptical and downright opposed to change, a situation that persists with such projects into the 21st century! There were those who claimed that horses would be frightened by electric trams, those who were concerned about unemployment as a result of new technology being adopted, and those who were honest enough to admit that their concerns were based upon perceived competition. Progress was not to be stopped however, and the first electric tramway opened in Dublin between Haddington Road and Dalkey in

1896. The line opened under the auspices of the Dublin South District Tramway (DSDT) and as it happens, the Dalkey route was the last survivor of the traditional tramway routes, finally succumbing in 1949.

The DUTC took over the DSDT in 1896 and the process of electrification continued until the era of the Dublin horse tram came to a close in 1900. At that time the Dublin tramways were quite profitable and there was particular demand from the middle classes. The first Irish-manufactured electric tram emerged from the DUTC's Spa Road Works in Inchicore in 1897. Tram production, and later bus production, continued there into the CIÉ period.

By the 1920s the DUTC's tram network covered a substantial portion of the city and comprised approximately 100 km of routes. There were a number of other tramway companies operating also at this time, two in west Dublin, the Dublin and Lucan Electric Tramway (DLET) and the Dublin and

Lucan Village in the early 1900s. It was in 1900 that the DLER commenced electric tram services between Lucan and Conyngham Road Dublin. Previously the route had been a 3-foot gauge steam tramway. The D&LER also carried some freight and a goods wagon may be seen behind the tram. *(Author's Collection)*

O'CONNELL STREET, DUBLIN

Blessington Steam Tramway (DBST). On the north side of the city, the Great Northern Railway operated the Hill of Howth Tramway.

The DUTC also played a significant part in Irish history other than from a transport perspective. The company was one of the city's largest employers and working conditions were not so good. Employees had to work long hours for low pay, but were afraid to complain as alternative work was very difficult to find. James Larkin, the pioneering Irish trade unionist, and the Irish Transport and General Workers Union, organised workers for a strike in August 1913, to force the DUTC to provide better pay and conditions of employment. Some 700 of the 1700 employees went out on strike. It wasn't long before discontent manifested itself elsewhere and by the end of the month 25,000 people were on strike, locked out by employers or unemployed. The troubles continued until January 1914 and eventually the stand-off ended; but another revolution ominously beckoned.

Despite the DUTC's infamy and the part the company played in the '1913 Lock-out' under the directorship of William Martin Murphy, the company was still successful and made good profits using new technology. The same could not be said for the Lucan tramway, which closed in 1925, to be followed by the Blessington tramway in 1932.

Nelson's Pillar in Dublin's O'Connell Street was not only effectively the city centre, but also the focal point for Dublin's tramway system. In this aerial view the remaining tram routes of the 1940s can be seen crossing Carlisle Bridge from the south side and terminating at the Pillar. Some redundant tracks can also be made out to the right of the Daniel O'Connell statue at the beginning of O'Connell Street. Like the tram tracks, the Pillar has also vanished. The site of the Pillar is now occupied by The Spire, which in the author's view looks like a large radio aerial. At least tram tracks will return to O'Connell Street in the near future. (Postcard in Author's Collection)

The Lucan Tramway

The Lucan tramway story is quite an interesting one as it started as a 3-foot gauge steam tramway in 1881, reached Lucan Village in 1883, and was extended to Leixlip in 1890. Like some other tramways of the day, it was more akin to a roadside light railway, with locomotives, passenger carriages and a goods service. Plans were mooted for extensions to Maynooth, Kilcock, Donaghdea, Hazelhatch and as far as Sallins, but none of these came to fruition. The extension to Leixlip only lasted nine years and by 1899, the whole route was closed for rebuilding into an electric tramway with a new gauge of 3 foot 6 inches.

To power the electric line a power house was constructed at Fonthill, and the building survives to this day, in use by a welding supplies company. The new electric tramway also provided a goods service and even had a special tram for conveying post. Despite the rebuilding, the tramway was to lead a short life in its new guise and had closed again by 1925. This was not the end of the story though, as it was to undergo another transformation. This time the DUTC built a standard gauge (5 feet 3 inches/1600 mm gauge) line on the route, complete with automatic colour-light signalling. Alas, the tramway lasted only 15 years in this guise, finally closing forever in 1940.

Lucan Village terminus DUTC route No 25 circa 1930s. *(Author's Collection)*

Dublin United Tramway Company

Regarding the DUTC itself, its routes eventually reached Kingstown (Dún Laoghaire), Dalkey, Donnybrook, Terenure, Landsdowne Road, Phoenix Park, Whitehall, Clonskeagh, Dartry, Dollymount, Howth, Rialto, Glasnevin, Inchicore, and as noted previously, Lucan. In effect, the vast majority of the city was within reach of a tram line, and most of the routes came together in the city centre at Nelson's Column on Sackville Street, now O'Connell Street. By the 1920s the DUTC fleet comprised around 300 trams. From 1925 the company started opening bus routes, signalling the eventual decline of the importance of the tram. The company also changed its name to the Dublin United *Transport* Company in March 1941, reflecting its diversification.

By the time that the Great Southern Railways and the DUTC amalgamated to form Córas Iompair Éireann in 1945, only the tram lines to Dalkey, Dartry and Terenure remained. All of these lines closed over the next few years, with the Dalkey line, the very last of the traditional tramways of the former DUTC, closing on 10 July 1949. The tramways remained a political issue well into the 1960s however, with mention being made in the Dáil (Parliament) from time to time, but it took until the 1990s until a decision was finally made to bring trams back to the capital.

When the Lucan tramway came back to life under the auspices of the DUTC, it had been totally rebuilt and connected to the main DUTC network at Parkgate Street. The newly rebuilt line even had colour-light signalling for the passing loops on the erstwhile single-track line. New trams were also built known as 'Lucan Standard Cars'. In this photograph a city-bound tram leaves Chapelizod Village. *(Leabharlann Náisiúnta na hÉireann)*

The Dublin and Blessington Steam Tramway

The Blessington tram was quite the poor cousin in comparison with the other Dublin tramways. Opened in 1888, the line commenced in Terenure and largely followed the road to Blessington some 25 km distant. Being of the same gauge as the DUTC it formed an end-on junction with that system in Terenure, and goods wagons were exchanged between the two systems at this point. DBST steam locomotives were not permitted into the city and haulage of the goods trains over the DUTC lines was by DUTC electric traction. The DBST line was extended from Blessington to Poulaphouca in 1895, and this extension closed in 1927 some five years before the main part of the route. The extension was actually built by a separate company, the Blessington and Poulaphouca Steam Tramway (BPST). Like the original Lucan line, there were some ambitious plans for extension that included such distant places as Rathdum via the Wicklow Gap and Glendalough. Further extensions did not happen however.

By 1914 the DBST was in financial trouble and when the Great Southern Railway came into being in 1924, the DBST was not invited, leaving it to soldier on alone, which amazingly it did for another eight years. At some point electrification of the DBST between Terenure and Crooksling was considered, with the plan being that the trams would continue on to Blessington using a petrol engine. There were insufficient resources available to the ailing company to pursue such plans, although experiments were carried out in 1915 with some petrol electric trams, but they were not a success. Another experimental form of traction, petrol railbuses, were also tried out in 1925. These were more successful and were used as far as Jobstown. Finally a larger Drewry Car Co petrol railcar was purchased and could carry up to 40 passengers. This was not enough to ward off bus competition however and the tramway finally expired in 1932.

Like the original Lucan tramway, the DBST had many of the features of a railway as opposed to a tramway. For the most part it had its own right of way, albeit roadside, and under the legislation under which it was constructed, it had to comply with tramway regulations. *(South Dublin Libraries Collection)*

Top: A petrol electric tram No 1 of the DBST. These were not a success. *(South Dublin Libraries Collection)*

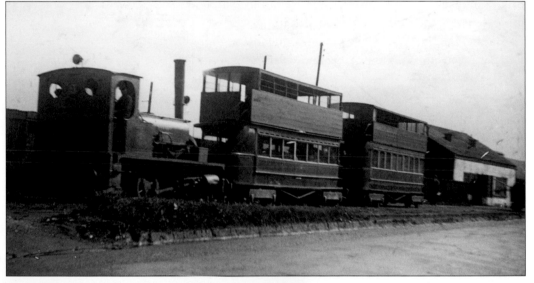

Centre: An 0-4-0ST of the DBST hauls two double deck tram cars at Templeogue. Note the lack of side-skirts on the loco and the extra tall funnel to clear the upper deck. *(South Dublin Libraries Collection)*

Left: The Poulaphouca terminus of the BPST line until 1927 is seen here in 1988. For a while this building served as a pub called 'The Tramway'. It is now a private dwelling and has since been beautifully restored. The current owners have it adorned with a period 'GSR Motor Bus Stops Here' sign. *(Dónal Murray)*

Hill of Howth Tramway

The Hill of Howth Tramway was without a shadow of doubt in a category of its own. Consisting of one single route, commencing at the GNR's Sutton Station, the line climbed Howth Head to a station at the summit. From the summit, the line then descended the other side of Howth Head to the GNR's Howth Station. The tramway was opened in 1901 by the GNR and was built to the same standard gauge as the railway. When the portion of the GNR that lay in Republic was taken over by CIÉ in 1958, CIÉ had divested itself of tramway operations, and must not have welcomed the acquisition of another. No time was wasted and the Hill of Howth Tramway was finally closed in 1959, leaving Dublin without a passenger tram until the arrival of the Luas in 2004.

The Hill of Howth tramway differed in a number of ways from the other public tramways, and particularly those of the former DUTC. One of these differences was that, despite a frequency of approximately every 20 minutes during the day, the tramway's passenger traffic was quite sparse outside of what we now term as peak commuting hours. Before 1959, the population of the district which the tramway served was quite low, and it was really only in the era when private car ownership began to increase that the population of the area grew. By this stage, it was too late for the tramway.

The last Howth tram in 1959. (*Leabharlann Náisiúnta na h-Éireann*)

The tramway did of course benefit considerably from tourist and leisure traffic during the summer, particularly at the weekends. It is a pity that there was not the foresight in 1959 to retain the tramway, even if only a summer schedule was operated for the benefit of tourists, as it would surely be a popular attraction today. The views across Dublin Bay and beyond are quite spectacular from Howth and the tram route offered some fine vistas.

As a last word regarding the Hill of Howth Tramway, it could be said that the tramway was ahead of its time when it came to communications. A maintenance tram that travelled the line was perhaps the first rail vehicle in Ireland with a mobile telephone! The telephone did however have to be physically plugged into one of the line-side telegraph poles to be used, and therefore it could be argued that it was actually a relocatable telephone and not a mobile one, but nonetheless, it was unique at the time.

Below: The Hill of Howth Tramway Depot at Sutton. *(Leabharlann Náisiúnta na h-Éireann)*

The Guinness Tramway

Another tramway existed in Dublin city that is worth a mention, the Guinness Brewery tramway. Although it was not a public tramway *per se*, it did occasionally carry passengers. The tramway, or tramways, as there were two distinct track gauges used, was built for the purpose of transporting the ingredients of the famous drink around the brewery. They were also used to transport the finished product in barrels either to the Quays for transport by barge to the Docks, or to Kingsbridge (Heuston) Station for onward rail transport around the country. A unique feature of the system was that some narrow gauge steam locomotives built for the system could be lifted into special adapter wagons so that they could be used on the standard gauge portions of the system.

In the final years of the tramway's existence, special trains were used to take tourists around the Brewery. The system finally succumbed in 1975, but some of the rails are still in place around the brewery and the surrounding streets to this day.

Above: The Guinness tramway narrow gauge. Adjacent to the River Liffey Guinness had a wharf from where barges carried the Guinness downstream to the docks for export. *(Seán Kennedy)*

Left: A standard gauge Hudswell diesel of the Guinness tramway on St John's Road outside Kingsbridge station. The line here connected the Brewery with Kingsbridge Yard. *(Des McGlynn)*

Reasons for the demise of the traditional tramways

The demise of tramways started as soon as other choices of motorised road transport started to become available. From a public transport perspective, it was much easier and economical to use buses, as there was no need to create special infrastructure. Routes could effectively be changed at will and to suit demand, something the tramways could not accommodate. It must be borne in mind that oil was also quite cheap in the early part of the 20th century, and pollution or environmental factors were not of immediate public concern.

Another factor that favoured buses was that it was relatively easy to purchase an 'off-the-shelf' bus, and create a new service parallel to a tramway, or anywhere for that matter. Cheaper than a bespoke tramcar, and without the cost of paying for or maintaining one's own road as a tramway company did, the likes of the DUTC could clearly see that this was the way to maintain profitability in an era when competition was growing. From 1925 onwards, the DUTC started putting buses on the road and planning the gradual abandonment of the tram routes. By the second half of the 20th century, the traditional tramways had all but disappeared from the city streets in Ireland and the UK. With the benefit of hindsight, the almost total abandonment of tramways in these islands was a mistake in the long term. Unfortunately it took almost 50 years for the 'Powers That Be' to come to this conclusion. That said, the traditional tramways differed considerably from modern systems not only in terms of technology, but in their entire concept. To be efficient, modern tramways require quite a degree of their own right of way and an infrastructure that can accommodate longer and faster vehicles.

CHAPTER 5

LUAS – LIGHT RAIL SYSTEM

The Luas Bridge at Taney Cross, Dundrum, under construction in February 2002. The embankment of the former Harcourt Street line had been obliterated by road construction. *(Dónal Murray)*

By the 1990s it was painfully obvious that the city of Dublin was gradually choking with motor traffic, and that things would only get worse if nothing was done. It was both ironic and tragic that this had all been predicted in the AM Voorhees report, commissioned by CIÉ in the early 1970s. The report had been studiously ignored by successive governments that were hell-bent on spending millions building new roads and moving the traffic problems from one place to another. Meanwhile, public transport, and particularly rail transport, was starved of investment. In April 1994, the Dublin Transport Initiative (DTI) published a report that suggested amongst other things that Dublin needed a three route, light rail system, to serve Tallaght, Ballymun and Cabinteely. Amazingly, the routes suggested were broadly in line with routes suggested as part of the Dublin Rapid Rail Transit plan of some 20 years before. The DTI estimated the cost of the system at £300 million (punt) in 1994 values.

In October 1994, the newly formed CIÉ Light Rail Project Office started planning the system in detail.

77

They proposed that the first line to be built should be to Dundrum/Ballally, largely upon the abandoned Harcourt Street line route, followed by the line from the city centre to Ballymun. It was then proposed the Dundrum/Ballally line should be extended to Sandyford Industrial Estate. In 1996 a new piece of legislation was enacted, The Dublin Light Rail Act, to create the legal framework to plan, construct and operate the proposed lines. Planning started in earnest in early 1997, but a change in government proved disastrous, and vested political interests ensured that yet another report suggested fundamental changes to the project. These changes, which set the project backwards considerably and resulted in substantial extra costs, also resulted in the abandonment of the Ballymun line and a city centre connection between the Sandyford and Tallaght routes. The separation of the routes meant that two depots were now required, one for each line. It is only now, in the second decade of the new millennium, that the city centre connection is finally underway. Ballymun unfortunately, was left out in the cold indefinitely.

For a period, the light rail system was made into something of a political football, but eventually the government decided to go ahead with two lines in 1998. Line A (later the Red Line) would run from Connolly Station, via Heuston Station to Tallaght, and Line B (later the Green Line), would run from St Stephen's Green to Sandyford Industrial Estate via Dundrum.

In 2000 the Railway Procurement Agency (RPA) was founded, and this organisation took over the role of CIÉ's Light Rail Project Office. In 2002 a contract was let out to Connex (later Veolia) for the operation of the light rail system, which by this stage had become known as the 'Luas', which is Irish language for speed. Another contract was let out to Alstom for the maintenance of the trams and infrastructure. One year later saw the trial of the first tram on the section of the line between the maintenance depot at The Red Cow and Tallaght. Early in 2004, the first tram crossed the impressive new cable-stayed bridge at Taney Road in Dundrum on the Green Line. The new bridge was required to link the two long-severed parts of the former Harcourt Street alignment. The year 2004, also saw the completion of the last section of rails at Connolly Station on the Red Line.

A Luas tram at the Dundrum stop. This was the location of the railway station on the former Harcourt Street line, closed in 1958. The former station building may be seen to the right. Directly behind the tram, heading towards the city the impressive and aptly named 'William Dargan Bridge' over Taney Road may be seen. (*Dónal Murray*)

With the lines in place, serious trials of the rolling stock and infrastructure commenced, and also a public safety awareness campaign. At 3:00 pm on 30 June 2004, the Green Line opened to the public between St Stephen's Green and Sandyford. Free travel was made available on the line for three days to promote the new line. The Red Line followed some months later and commenced operations between Tallaght and Connolly Station on 28 October 2004.

Left: Infrastructure construction work underway on the Red Line at Ballymount in 2002. It had been more than 100 years since a completely new public tramway had been constructed in the city, but even at this stage there were commentators that accused the government of wasting money on a 'white elephant' project. The subsequent success of the Luas disproved such ludicrous accusations. *(Dónal Murray)*

The control room at the Red Cow Depot in December 2002, with construction work still underway. *(Dónal Murray)*

A brand new Citadis 301 series Luas tram, still with bubble wrap on the seats inside, at the Red Cow Depot, December 2002. *(Dónal Murray)*

The Red Line

The Luas Red Line was opened in October 2004, and from 28 October, there were some six days of free travel to publicise the new service. The construction of this line benefited from some European Union funding to the tune of €82.5 million. The line itself differs significantly from the Green Line, in particular because its infrastructure is not largely based upon the route of a former segregated railway line and has quite a number of street running sections and at-grade crossings. As a result of these differences, there were a number of safety issues relatively unique to the Red Line, and a well thought out public safety awareness campaign was required. Unfortunately, despite this initial and subsequent campaigns, the Red Line has experienced and continues to experience, a number of incidents, in particular involving road vehicles running red lights or obstructing the right of way. One of the most serious incidents occurred at the junction of O'Connell Street and Abbey Street in 2009 when a tram collided with a Dublin Bus. On this occasion, the road vehicle had not run the lights, but in most instances it has been the lack of care on the part of motorists that is the problem.

Another difference between the Red and Green Lines is the length of the trams themselves. Initially and rather bizarrely, it was planned that shorter vehicles in the 301 series would be used on the Red Line. Almost immediately following the opening of the line, it was apparent that the trams lacked sufficient capacity for the route and Connex and the RPA recognised that it would be necessary to lengthen the vehicles. By 2010 all of the Red Line's 301 series trams had extra sections added to give an equivalent capacity to the Green Line's 401 series trams.

Left: A Citadis 401 series unit on test at Sandyford in March 2004.
(Dónal Murray)

Top: A busy moment at the Red Line Red Cow stop and Depot in summer 2010. The unit on the right has just off loaded its passengers and is coming out of service, whilst a following service to Tallaght has just arrived. (Dónal Murray)

Above: The Luas line to Citywest under construction in 2009. (Railway Procurement Agency)

Right: A lengthened Citadis 301 series tram on the Red Line at the Saggart Luas terminus, opened in July 2010. *(Dónal Murray)*

Below: A Citadis 401 series Luas tram at Stillorgan on the Green Line in 2005. *(Dónal Murray)*

The Green Line

As has already been noted, the Green Line is largely built along the alignment of the former Harcourt Street line. The Harcourt Street Line ran from a terminus at the end of Harcourt Street to Bray via Dundrum, and the line was closed in 1958 just as the areas that it passed through were being developed. At the time CIÉ was struggling financially and had an obligation from the government to reach profitability once again, something it had not achieved since nationalisation. With rail closures taking place all around the country, the capital could not be spared and in any event, CIÉ believed that buses could adequately serve the areas that the Harcourt Street line ran through.

The closure of the route, the hasty dismantling of bridges and divesting of the infrastructure, remained a source of controversy for a generation. As the surrounding suburbs grew, with traffic congestion growing in tandem, calls for the reopening continued but fell on deaf ears. The first glimmer of hope came following the AM Voorhees report of the early 1970s as previously mentioned. The Dublin Rail Rapid Transit plans also showed a proposed busway on the former Harcourt Street alignment to Dundrum. Alas, as we have seen, the Dublin Rapid Transit plan was never implemented in any sort of coherent or timely manner due to continued political indifference and vested interests. There were also physical barriers to the reconstruction of a rail line and, whilst not completely insurmountable, they would add significant extra costs to any project and a considerable degree of planning would be required. Following CIÉ's hasty destruction of the line, a number of developments had taken place across the original alignment, both in the city and the outer suburbs. Some of these developments had been carried out without planning permission, but nonetheless were still in the way. Thankfully, Dublin County Council had managed to preserve the bulk of

A week after the public opening of The Green Line in 2004, a tram waits its turn at Sandyford. (*Dónal Murray*)

Luas units on test on the Red Line extension to The Point in 2009. *(Railway Procurement Agency)*

The way ahead. The driver's view from the tram under test at Mayor Street, on the line to The Point in 2009. *(Railway Procurement Agency)*

Above: Two Luas trams on trial at Mayor Street, on the extension of the Red Line to The Point in 2009. *(Railway Procurement Agency)*

Left: Engineers check clearances between a Luas tram and a platform on the extension line to The Point in 2009. *(Railway Procurement Agency)*

the alignment but perhaps the most significant obstacle was a new road junction at Taney in Dundrum that had completely obliterated a huge section of the original alignment and would require a very substantial bridge to span the gap created by the new road formation.

Finally common sense prevailed with the 'Powers That Be' and it was decided that the line would be reopened in a new guise as a light rail line, but this time commencing closer to the city centre at St Stephen's Green, heading south on Harcourt Street more or less on the route of an old tramway that had existed there until 1948, regaining the old Harcourt Street alignment just beyond the former rail terminus itself, and continuing more or less along the old rail alignment as far as Sandyford, directly adjacent to the former Stillorgan railway station. The crossing of the road junction at Taney in Dundrum would require a bridge with a very large clear span whilst maintaining the rigidity required for rail vehicles, and a rather spectacular cable-stayed bridge design was chosen. Following a competition, the bridge was named 'William Dargan Bridge' in honour of the great pioneering Irish railway engineer of the 1800s.

Success of the Luas

When the Luas light rail system was being planned, there was considerable comment in the media about the project being something of the fabled 'white elephant', and that there would be no be difference to traffic congestion as a result. According to such commentators the new system would just be another burden on the taxpayer and, worse still, some claimed quite spuriously that city centre businesses would face huge losses as a result of construction. The proposed gauge difference between the Luas and the DART was also raised as an issue. The Luas would be built to

June 2004 and despite the Luas Green Line now being in public operation, some finishing work is still required at the Ranelagh stop. *(Dónal Murray)*

international standard gauge of 1435 mm as against the Irish standard of 1600 mm. Much was made of the perceived lack of interchangeability of the two systems and the gauge debate was almost reminiscent of the beginnings of Irish railways.

As soon as Luas services commenced, the arguments against the system quickly evaporated. Just like the DART some 20 years before, commuters immediately took to the new high-quality rail-based system. Defying predictions, significant numbers of these commuters were formerly car commuters. Further defying the critics, the Luas broke even and started to be profitable sooner than had been expected.

Reverting to the gauge issue, the Luas planners had good reason to choose the international standard gauge of 1435 mm over the Irish standard gauge of 1600 mm. The use of international standard gauge enabled the RPA to order off-the-shelf vehicles instead of having to get them made to a relatively unique gauge at additional expense. It would also enable the vehicles to have some sort of re-sale value to other systems abroad when they would eventually be replaced by newer units on the Luas system. The ability to link up with the DART or heavy rail system was never a real consideration, as traditionally light and heavy rail systems do not mix due to different infrastructural and safety requirements. There are of

course exceptions to this in some countries but the modal interchanges that have been created between the Luas and Iarnród Éireann systems clearly show that there never was a need for the two systems' trackwork to physically connect.

With the obvious success of the Luas and the slick modern image of the new transport system, came the predictable demand that the system be expanded to serve other areas. Almost immediately the RPA started to plan additional lines.

It was a justifiable source of controversy that the two lines were not only physically separated in the city centre but that there was actually a 15 minute walk required if one was to attempt to make use of the two lines for a journey. A city centre link was of course originally envisaged as part of the never-built Ballymun line, but some Dublin business interests and politicians had ensured that the city centre link was put onto the back burner and by extension had kyboshed the line to Ballymun completely. The lack of vision of these parties was quite astounding, as experience overseas had proved that light rail systems aided a city's regeneration and ultimately improved business in general. However, although the crucial link between the two lines was destined to be a least a decade into the future, the city would see an expansion of the system in the shorter term.

The current terminus of the Green Line at St Stephen's Green with a Citadis 402 series tram. *(Des McGlynn)*

With the first two lines in place, attention turned to Dublin's Docklands, an area that had rapidly expanded but was largely bereft of public transport. By extending the Red Line eastwards from Connolly Station this area could be served, whilst on the far side of the city the large Citywest Business campus was seeking a branch off the Red Line and the developers of the campus were willing to contribute towards the costs. The Green Line was not to be left out either, and an extension from Sandyford to Cherrywood was envisaged, also with the aid of developer contribution. Although the destination of this particular extension lay on the former Harcourt Street alignment, the RPA planned to deviate from the old route to serve more populous recent housing developments, which was a most sensible decision. Therefore from Sandyford to Carrickmines the line followed a completely new alignment and required two bridges over the orbital M50 motorway.

With plans for the extension of the Red and Green Lines in hand, the RPA let out a contract in March 2007, worth some €51 million for 18 new vehicles. Following on from this an order was placed for a further 8 vehicles worth €22 million. These vehicles were required to maintain the current frequency of the existing services and those of the extensions to The Point (Docklands/Line C1), Citywest (Line A1), and Cherrywood (Line B1). The first new trams in the Citadis 402 series started to arrive from February 2009 and all are now in service.

The new trams brought the fleet to a total of 66 vehicles, with 26 on the Green Line and 40 on the Red Line. The newest trams, the Citadis 402 series are 43 m in length, somewhat longer than their predecessors, and this required some extensions to the Depots. As the Red Line's 301 series units had also been extended to 40 m, the Red Cow Depot had to be extended in any event.

A 401 series leaves Stillorgan bound for St Stephen's Green along the old Harcourt Street alignment in 2003. *(Dónal Murray)*

Left: A substantial curved bridge was required in Sandyford Industrial Estate to carry the Green Line extension to Cherrywood across a complex road junction. *(Railway Procurement Agency)*

Below: Cut and cover tunnel construction at Spine Road on the Green Line extension to Cherrywood. *(Railway Procurement Agency)*

Right: Carrickmines was a country station on the DSER's Harcourt Street to Bray route. When the line closed in 1958 the station building like others on the line, became a private residence. In August 2002 the former station building remained in a relatively traquill setting, whilst a few kilometres further north, the Sandyford to Harcourt Road section of the former railway was in the process of being 'dusted off' for use as what was to become the Luas Green Line. *(Dónal Murray)*

Below: Ten years later in December 2012, the station building is derelict but a double track rail line has returned! Carrickmines now has a stop on the Cherrywood extension of the Luas Green Line. *(Dónal Murray)*

The Green Line Cherrywood extension opened on 16 October 2010, the Red Line extension to The Point in Dublin's Docklands opened on 8 December 2010, and the Red Line branch to Citywest opened on 2 July 2011.

In 2007, three years after the opening of the first two lines, there were some 28.4 million journeys on the Luas, an increase of 10% on the previous year. By European standards this was quite high, and exceeded even the DART's passenger level increase. The Red Line was the bigger carrier of the two, with some 15.8 million journeys compared with the Green Line's 12.6 million. The busiest day of 2007 was 21 December with 145,000 passengers in one day.

One thing was proved beyond a shadow of doubt, the Luas was not a 'white elephant'! Quite the opposite in fact. Claims of negative effects on city centre businesses had also been completely disproved although spurious claims would arise again when the planning of the city centre link started again some time later.

Our final view of Carrickmines shows a Luas 402 series tram heading north for St Stephen's Green. The Luas destination displays alternate between the Irish and English language versions and it is the Irish version of St Stephen's Green that may be seen on the tram. In the distance is a new road over-bridge that replaced the original one whose cast iron parapet is just visible in the 2002 view of Carrickmines Station. *(Dónal Murray)*

End of the Green Line (for the time being at least) at Cherrywood in September 2012. *(Jake Murray)*

CHAPTER 6
METRO FOR DUBLIN

Metro North

Metro North forms part of the envisioned integrated light rail system for the capital, a network that commenced with the opening of the Green and Red Luas Lines. The 'Metro' name is a bit of misnomer in technical terms, for what is proposed does not fall into the category of Metros such as Paris or London (Underground), nor would it have the capacity of say the DART line. What is actually proposed is broadly similar to the Luas lines but with a greater degree of segregation from other traffic, allowing longer and faster vehicles to use the line. This will be achieved by running the Metro line underground in the city centre, and grade separating intersections with road traffic on the outskirts of the city. In short, the Metro line should have an uninterrupted right of way.

Metro North is planned to commence at St Stephen's Green, where there will be an interchange with the existing Luas Green Line and a future Iarnród Éireann DART Interconnector. The line will head north, with underground stations at O'Connell Bridge (interchange with Luas Red Line), Parnell Square,

A computer generated image of the Swords Metro stop. The principal difference between the Metro and the Luas is that the Metro will be totally on its own right of way and grade-separated at junctions. This will enable higher speeds and longer vehicles which will greatly increase capacity. *(Railway Procurement Agency)*

Top: Dublin is one of the few western European capital cities that does not have its principal Airport rail connection to the city centre. This will change with the arrival of Metro North's Airport stop. *(Railway Procurement Agency)*

Centre: A computer generated image of the O'Connell Bridge stop. The underground stop at O'Connell Bridge will provide an interchange with the Luas Red Line and local bus services. Likewise, the underground stop at St Stephen's Green will provide an interchange with Luas Green Line and Iarnród Éireann DART services, the latter via the Interconnector. *(Railway Procurement Agency)*

Left: To facilitate the future construction of the Metro North Mater Station, and to prevent delays to the ongoing extension of the Mater Hospital, it was necessary to install a diaphragm wall at the site in 2012, even though the Metro project itself has been long-fingered. In the photo, civil engineering work is seen underway at the future station site on a very wet day in June 2012. *(Railway Procurement Agency)*

Mater Hospital, Drumcondra (interchange with Iarnród Éireann Maynooth line), Griffith Avenue, and Dublin City University. Emerging above ground, there will be stations at Ballymun, Santry, Metropark, Dublin Airport (underground), Nevinstown, Swords, Seatown, and terminating at Lissenhall.

It is expected that some 34 million passengers per annum will use Metro North, and passengers will be able to travel from Dublin Airport to the city centre within 18 minutes, or from Swords within 26 minutes. Metro trains will operate on a 4 minute frequency in peak-hours and passengers will easily be able to interchange with Iarnród Éireann, Metro West, Luas and bus services. With some 2000 'Park and Ride' spaces made available and the aforementioned interchanges, it is expected that Metro North will have a significant impact in reducing motor traffic, with a prediction of removing approximately 100 million road vehicle journeys per annum.

Metro West

Metro West differs from almost all of the other light rail and heavy rail plans for the city in that it is an orbital route, and is one the few proposals that bears little or no resemblance to any of the lines envisaged as part of the CIÉ Rapid Rail Transit scheme back in the 1970s. The concept of Metro West is that Dublin has expanded to such an extent that commuters do not just make radial journeys anymore (ie into and out of the city centre). Many commuters travel to work not just across town but around it, as is evidenced by the orbital M50 motorway and other ring roads at peak hours. Therefore there is, and has been for some time, a need for an orbital rail line to provide commuters with more travel options and to link up the various radial lines.

Unlike Metro North, Metro West, as of 2012, was not near construction stage, but is practically fully planned with the route chosen, etc. Also, unlike

At Belgard, near Tallaght, the Metro West stop will be situated on a bridge spanning a busy intersection and the Luas Red Line. The existing Luas Red Line stop, where the lines to Tallaght and Citywest diverge, is seen in the top right hand corner of the image. At the time of writing, it has had its distinctive white sail canopies removed. *(Railway Procurement Agency)*

Metro West's proposed Fonthill stop will form an interchange with Iarnród Éireann's Fonthill Station on the Kildare line. A large car park has already been built at the location to the right of the image and the area to the left as far as Iarnród Éireann's Kishogue Station is to be developed for high density housing. *(Railway Procurement Agency)*

The proposed Quarryvale Stop near to Liffey Valley Shopping Centre will be built in a cutting, as Metro West will have to pass under the proposed Lucan Luas line, some busy road intersections and the N4 dual carriageway, before crossing the Liffey Valley on a new bridge. *(Railway Procurement Agency)*

Metro North, Metro West will not feature extensive underground sections due to the greater availability of land for a surface right-of way in the outer suburbs. It will however be largely segregated from road traffic and will have some significant grade-separated junctions.

Metro West will commence at Tallaght at an interchange with the Luas Red Line, which it will intersect with again at Belgard, also giving an interchange with the City West Red Line branch. The line will then continue on to Clondalkin, Fonthill (Interchange with Iarnród Éireann Kildare line) and Quarryvale (for Liffey Valley), where there will be an interchange with the Luas Lucan line. The line will then cross the River Liffey Valley on a substantial bridge, reaching Porterstown, where there will be an interchange with Iarnród Éireann's Maynooth line, before serving the Blanchardstown Centre and carrying on to a junction with Metro North near to the Airport. 'Park and Ride' facilities will be situated at stops close to major road junctions, along with cycle parking facilities. The location of the lines' depot will be on the north side of the Liffey, either at Abbotstown, Porterstown or Silogue.

There were some serious environmental impact concerns with regard to the crossing of the Liffey Valley by Metro West on a new bridge. An architectural competition was launched to get the best design and was won by Buro Hapold and Explorations Architecture. In the author's humble opinion, the design of this bridge is far superior aesthetically to that of the M50 orbital motorway a short distance downstream. It is planned that there will also be a public walkway deck incorporated into the bridges. The bridge will be 350 m in length and 17 m wide. *(Railway Procurement Agency)*

CHAPTER 7

FUTURE OF THE RAILWAYS: TO NAVAN (AGAIN?)

Navan (GNR) station seen here in the 1970s. Passenger trains, except for the odd GAA special, had long ceased to call at this stage. Freight traffic from Tara Mines and gypsum from Kingscourt remained however. Gypsum traffic from Kingscourt finally ceased in 1999. *(Des McGlynn)*

Train services to Navan from the MGWR's Broadstone terminus, via Clonsilla commenced in 1862. During 'The Emergency' (the Second World War), passenger train services on the line were suspended and then withdrawn completely in 1947 during the fuel crisis brought about by the severe winter. A goods service and special trains continued to use the increasingly run-down line until 1963, when the line closed completely. CIÉ wasted little time in lifting the line and selling off the land. To be fair to the company and the 'Powers That Be' of the day, there was not sufficient demand for the line to be viable at the time, and the hinterland was sparsely populated. Like the Harcourt Street line however, it was known around the time of closure, that Dublin's suburbs would expand out towards County Meath and Dunboyne in the future, and likewise, it was believed that the road system could adequately handle the future traffic.

By the year 2000, Dunboyne had long graduated from being a rural village to an outlying satellite town of the capital. Navan, the county town of County Meath had quite simply sprawled and it too was a dormitory town for the capital to a great extent. Traffic congestion on the N3 national trunk road to Navan had reached crisis point and despite plans for a somewhat controversial new motorway, it was clear that something else was required to relieve the pressure.

The Dublin Transportation Office (DTO) proposed that the section of the former Navan line between Clonsilla and Dunboyne be reopened, and Meath County Council came out in support of the idea. A study was commissioned and concluded that there was a good economic case for reopening this section of line to Dunboyne, and beyond for a short distance to a Park and Ride facility to be built adjacent to the proposed M3 motorway. At the beginning of 2008, Iarnród Éireann obtained a Railway Order and construction work commenced at the end of 2008. Work also started on building a new station at Docklands adjacent to the former GSWR and LNWR North Wall Yards. The plan was that the additional services from Pace (M3 Park and Ride) would operate via Dunboyne, a new station at Hansfield, Clonsilla and would then follow the former MGWR freight line non-stop to Docklands. Interchange would be provided at Clonsilla with Maynooth to Pearse services.

The line opened to much fanfare on 2 September 2010, and the author was fortunate enough to be invited by Iarnród Éireann to the official opening.

The previous year Iarnród Éireann commenced public consultation regarding opening the rest of the former MGWR route to Navan. Various studies had already been carried out and the 34 km long route would have a least four stations at Dunshaughlin, Kilmessan, Navan (Town) and Navan (North), the

The old station at Dunboyne in 1988, 25 years after the railway was closed completely and with almost the same period to wait before the arrival of another train. *(Dónal Murray)*

latter on the existing but closed Kingscourt line. Dunshaughlin was never on the original Navan line so a deviation from the original route would be required. The plan was that the line would be opened by 2015 under the general transport plan titled 'Transport 21'. However, Ireland was just about to slide from an economic slowdown into an economic catastrophe.

In the meantime, work had commenced on the controversial M3 motorway. Strangely, no consideration was given to the fact that the rail line would not only be cheaper to build, but would also have a greater capacity for carrying commuters, with less damage to the environment.

Dunboyne Station on the Official re-opening day 2 September 2010. The original station building seen in the last photograph is just out of sight to the left of this image, derelict. *(Dónal Murray)*

Left: The first passengers enter the M3 Parkway station situated at a Park and Ride facility next to the M3 Motorway. *(Dónal Murray)*

Below: Hansfield Station just before the line opened to the public in 2010. The opening of the station was delayed due to an issue with a developer over the provision of a station access road. It finally opened in 2013. *(Dónal Murray)*

The DART underground or the Dublin Interconnector is to be the second principal DART route in the city, although this time there will be a completely 'new-build' route involved. The new route will vastly increase DART and commuter rail capacity by freeing-up the existing bottlenecks and creating whole new journey possibilities. The Interconnector is part of an overall plan that will see a quite massive extension of electrified DART services, to such locations as Maynooth and Kildare. In addition to creating a far more integrated commuter rail network, The Interconnector will also have interchanges with the Luas and Metro. The core of the project is the 5.2 km tunnel that will link the Kildare commuter route from Inchicore with the Northern and Western commuter routes at Docklands. Intermediate stations will be located at Pearse Station (interchange with existing DART line), St Stephen's Green (interchange with Luas and Metro North), Christchurch, and Heuston Station (Interchange with Intercity services).

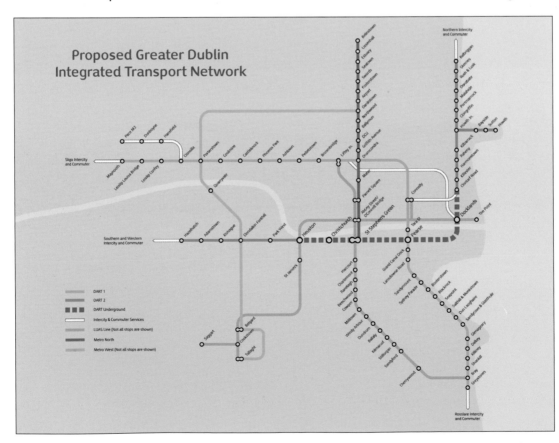

Map showing the Interconnector illustrating the interchanges with other rail services.
(Iarnród Éireann)

In addition to the investment made in the Kildare Route Project and with resignalling in the city centre, the Interconnector will increase the capacity of the Iarnród Éireann commuter lines to some 100 million passenger journeys per year. With the Interconnector in place it is planned that DART/commuter services from Maynooth/Navan will operate via Connolly Station to Bray and Greystones. DART services from Malahide/Howth will operate via Clontarf Road to Docklands and the Interconnector tunnel to Pearse Station and on to Kildare.

The tunnel will be constructed using a tunnel boring machine (TBM). Two single bore tunnels will be required with cross-passage escape/maintenance tunnels at intervals between them. The tunnel portals will be located at Inchicore and North Wall, and it is estimated that the tunnel will be an average of 20 m deep.

The method of station construction will depend upon the depth of the locations and what obstructions lie beneath ground level at those sites. Stations that are not at a very deep level may be constructed using 'cut and cover' methods whereas deep level stations will be constructed by expansion of the tunnel bores. All stations will be accessible to the mobility impaired and located close to other transport modes.

The original plan was that the DART Interconnector would be completed by 2015 during the term of the Transport 21 investment programme, but although substantial progress has been made with the planning and consultation for the project, the current economic state of the country has put paid to many vital projects in the short to medium term and the government has long-fingered the project. With geo-technical studies carried out, and public consultation completed, the plan was that following the receipt of a Railway Order in 2009, construction would start in 2010, some three years ago now. One can only hope that this project will not go the way of the Dublin Rapid Rail Transit plan of the 1970s that first envisaged such an underground interconnector.

Image of the DART underground. *(Iarnród Éireann)*

CHAPTER 9
FUTURE LUAS PLANS

Luas to Lucan (Line F)

It took 60 years for the Lucan area to get a train service back and it will be a much longer wait for Lucan to get a tram service back. However, plans have been made to do just that, as the RPA have been working on the design for the Lucan route for some time now. Back in 1940 when the Lucan tram closed, Lucan itself was little more than a village. In the 21st century, Lucan has a population of approximately 38,000, and has suffered more than its fair share of traffic congestion. Route options for a Lucan Luas line were presented to the community in September 2007, and by the end of October 2008 the RPA announced that the preferred route for Line F to Lucan had been chosen.

The Lucan line is planned to commence from a terminus on the Newcastle Road near to the Superquinn shopping centre in Lucan, and from there will head towards the city serving the housing estates of Esker, Castle Riada and Ballyowen. There will be an interchange with Metro West at Quarryvale, close to Liffey Valley. From there the line will continue towards the Liffey Valley shopping centre, where there may be two stops to serve the complex. From Liffey Valley, the line will continue on through Ballyfermot before turning onto the Kylemore Road and heading south as far as the Grand Canal, where it will turn towards the city again to run alongside the Canal to a junction with the Red Line at Black Horse, Inchicore. Line F will

The city centre link as originally envisaged in early Luas promotional literature in the 1990s. Westmoreland Street is seen here with two running lines. *(Author's collection)*

diverge again from the Red Line at Fatima, making its own way down Thomas Street to Christchurch and Dame Street. The finished line will be approximately 15 km long and is planned to have its own depot, although the location of the depot has not been confirmed as of yet. That said, back in 2009, when the Irish language version of this book was first written, it was estimated by the RPA that the Lucan line would be finished by 2013. The economic disaster wreaked upon Ireland by greedy bankers, developers, incompetent politicians and foreign loan sharks has put paid to the Lucan line for the foreseeable future however.

If and when the Lucan line finally gets the go ahead, it is planned that the trams that use the line will be 53 m long and will take 43 minutes to travel from Lucan to the city centre.

City Centre to Broombridge (Line BXD)

One of the most obvious faults with the current Luas system is that as a result of political interference with the project in its early days, the Red and Green Lines are not connected by any means. It had of course been planned that a third line, from Ballymun to St Stephen's Green would form such a link in the city centre.

Top: Liffey Junction circa 1975. A single 121 class No B125 heads for the city with a Sligo train past a line of redundant wagons. This location was once a hive of activity for freight and was the junction between the original MGWR main line from Broadstone and the MGWR route to North Wall, which also connected to the GSWR line at Glasnevin. A short distance behind the signal is the location of the present day Broombridge Station, which is not one of Iarnród Éireann's finest examples at present. The future for this location is bright however, as Luas's cross-city line, Line BXD, will form an interchange with Iarnród Éireann services at this location. *(Des McGlynn)*

Right: A nearly new two-car 2600 class unit passes the site of Liffey Junction on a Maynooth Service in 1995. To the right of the old MGWR water tower is the trackbed to Broadstone, soon to be part of the Luas line to and from the city centre to Broombridge, just behind the photographer. *(Des McGlynn)*

Instead, it is believed that some of the funding for this project was reallocated to allow the construction an minor bypass road in another constituency. Pressure from misinformed city business interests also played a part in the initial loss of a city centre connection.

One of the few transport projects that has survived a mothballing due to Ireland's current economic state, is however Line BXD. This line, which is planned to link the city centre with Broombridge, will finally provide that vital link between the existing lines in addition to other interchanges. The line will run from the Green Line at St Stephen's Green, where eventually there will be a junction with Iarnród Éireann's Interconnector and Metro North, down Dawson

Street and around College Green. At College Green, the North and Southbound running lines will split, with the northbound line running up Westmoreland Street and O'Connell Street. The line will cross the Red Line at O'Connell Street and will meet the southbound running line again at Parnell Square. The Southbound running line will reach College Green by heading south down Malborough Street and crossing the River Liffey on a new bridge, which is currently under construction, before continuing down Hawkins Street and back onto College Green.

Heading north from Parnell Square, the line will proceed up Dominick Street and on to Broadstone, passing by and around the former MGWR terminus,

Seen here in 2002, this track bed was closed to passengers in 1937 when services on the former MGWR lines to the west were transferred from Broadstone to Westland Row (now Pearse Station). It was almost involved in a 'turf dispute' between Iarnród Éireann and the Railway Procurement Agency (RPA) as both organisations had an eye on it for future use. Eventually it was decided that the RPA plan to use the track bed for Luas line BXD from Broombridge to St Stephen's Green via the city centre would go ahead, although Broadstone Station building itself does not feature as part of the plan. *(Dónal Murray)*

How the new bridge linking Marlbourogh Street and Hawkins Street will look, carrying the Luas BXD southbound line from Broombridge to St Stephen's Green. *(Railway Procurement Agency)*

with a stop serving the new Dublin Institute of Technology's campus at Grangegorman. The line will then use the alignment of the former MGWR main line, with a stop at Phibsborough, finally terminating at an interchange with an Iarnród Éireann's Maynooth line at Broombridge. A possible extension of the line to Finglas may be built at some future stage.

Cherrywood to Bray and Fassaroe (Line B2)

This extension was envisaged in happier days and therefore is unlikely to happen anytime soon, due to Ireland's current economic situation. Numerous proposals had been put forward for extension of the Cherrywood line to Bray, something that was quite natural, bearing in mind that the former Harcourt Street line had once done exactly that, via Shankill. Bray is served by the DART line, but has, like many satellite towns, sprawled over the years. Outlying areas such as Fassaroe have also expanded, without the benefit of adequate public transport services in some instances. Either Bray or Fassaroe were deemed worthy of extensions of the Cherrywood line, but one line serving both was not a practical solution from both a cost and travelling time point of view. As a result, the RPA came up with a plan for a line that would split into two.

The plan is to construct a line approximately 8.7 km long that will extend from Cherrywood as far as Shanganagh, splitting there into two branches. One branch will continue on to the DART station at Bray, whilst the other will serve Fassaroe, where a Park and Ride facility is planned. It was originally envisaged that the line would be constructed within the life of the Transport 21 plan, but this will not now happen, and it is anyone's guess as to when, if ever, the line will go ahead.

Luas to Rathfarnham and/or Metro South-West? (Line E)

In 2008, a study was carried out regarding a Luas line from Broadstone, from an interchange with line BXD through Harold's Cross, Terenure, Churchtown, to Dundrum, where there would be an interchange with the Luas Green Line, and on to Rathfarnham and Nutgrove. The line would be 9.8 km long. Back in 2001, the Dublin Transportation Office (DTO) had also envisaged a similar route as a possibility, as part of a line from Whitehall to Dundrum.

There were some issues with the plan however, other than economic ones: Constitution Hill near Broadstone presented a steep gradient and there were also some land acquisition problems. Perhaps more importantly, even in 2008 the RPA did not believe that there was a sufficient economic case for the line. The current economic situation suggests that this line is unlikely to become a live project for the next few decades, if ever.

South-West Luas/Metro/BRT

A planned rapid transit route from the city centre via Harold's Cross is, like many of the actual or proposed developments that we have seen, not an entirely new thing. The CIÉ Rapid Transit plan had envisaged a busway along the lines of the Runcorn Busway between the city centre, Harold's Cross, Kimmage and Tallaght. This proposal has since resurfaced in a number of guises.

The 2001 DTO report 'A Platform for Change' illustrated a Metro line running underground from the city centre (Tara Street) to Harold's Cross and Mount Argus via St Stephen's Green, and on the surface from Kimmage to Tallaght West via Wellington and Tymon. Broadly speaking, this route still remains part of the plans contained in the Greater Dublin Area Draft Transport Strategy of the National Transport Authority (NTA). However, it remains unclear what form the transit route may actually take along this corridor. At present it appears that a Luas line would be the preferred option but, like some of the currently stalled schemes, the Bus Rapid Transit option is also being explored. Whichever option is eventually taken up, the strategy recognises that some form of rapid transit is required along this corridor as the current bus services are hampered and frequently delayed by congestion and lack of comprehensive bus priority.

Map from the Dublin Transport Office report 'A Platform for Change' 2001. The south-west transit route is once again on the map in the form of a Metro line on this occasion. *(National Transport Authority)*

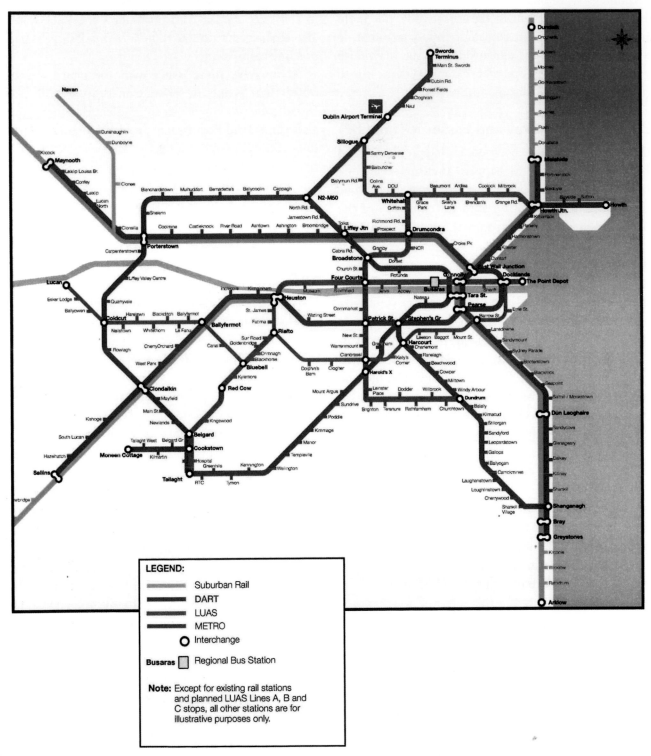

CHAPTER 10
ANOTHER FORM OF 'TRACKS FOR THE CITY'

The CIÉ Rapid Transit Plan of the 1970s, as has been mentioned previously, was not just about electrified heavy rail lines, but busways too. Two routes had originally been proposed, to Tallaght, via Harold's Cross, Mount Argus and Kimmage, and the other to Dundrum via the former Harcourt Street route. There was mention again of busways over the years and particularly in the late 1980s when the then Transport Minister mooted a possible re-opening of the Harcourt Street route, part of which lay in his constituency. This later route, as we have seen, became the Luas Green Line. The idea of busways has not gone away however, as we have seen in the last chapter.

The 1970s vision of a busway was little more than a completely segregated roadway for buses, such as that created in Runcorn, England. The concept has its merits of course. Buses can travel faster and are not hindered by other traffic. Buses are also more efficient

A guided Busway in the median of a busy road in Leeds. *(Courtesy West Yorkshire Passenger Transport Executive)*

from an urban transport perspective in terms of passenger-carrying capacity than other road vehicles, and pollution per passenger kilometre, but they do not have anywhere near the capacity of a light rail system and some statistics would suggest that the

A recently-opened example of a guided busway in Cambridgeshire, England. An unguided busway was part of the original CIÉ Rapid Transit Plan for the City Centre – Harold's Cross – Tallaght route. Could this be a more suitable alternative to the currently proposed Luas line? *(Cambridgeshire County Council)*

A Wright-built 'Streetcar' BRT Vehicle. *(The Wright Group)*

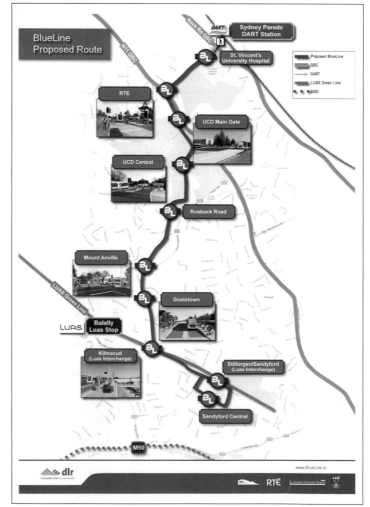

actual operating cost per passenger kilometre may be higher than light rail. That said, buses are somewhat more flexible as is evidenced by the story of the traditional tramways. Like everything else however, buses and busways have evolved, and Bus Rapid Transit is a reality, which can also take on a number of forms.

Guided busways have advanced considerably beyond the early experiments, and the O-Bahn guided busway concept in Adelaide, Australia is no longer so unique. Recently a guided busway has opened up in Cambridgeshire, England, much of it based upon an abandoned railway route. This project has aroused some international interest, and other cities in England and Europe have either considered, or even built somewhat similar systems. The Cambridge example is the world's longest section of guided busway and is effectively an interurban route.

In Dublin, and prior to the recent expansion in remit of the RPA into the BRT field, there has already been a proposal for a BRT route, between Sandymount and Sandyford. The route, known as the 'Blue Line', has been promoted by Dún Laoghaire Rathdown Council and Sandyford Business Estates Association, amongst other groups. The plan is to provide interchanges with

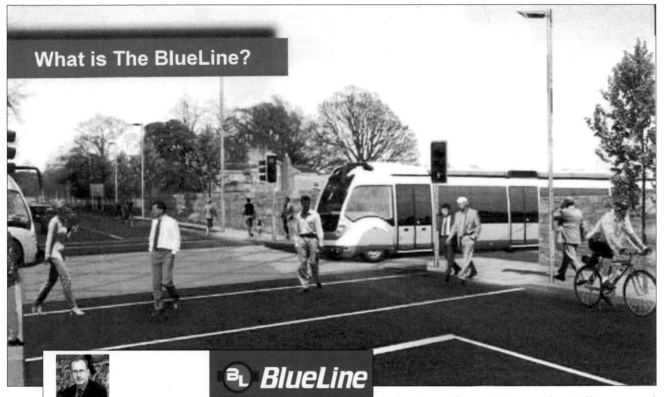

What is The BlueLine?

the Luas Green Line at the Stillorgan and Kilmacud stops and also serve University College Dublin at Belfield, and St Vincent's Hospital. At the N11 trunk road and Rock Road there would be interchanges with quality bus corridors (QBCs). The vehicles proposed would be basically articulated buses that look like light rail vehicles, similar to those used in some cities in the UK and US. The system would however be unguided. Instead it would have a dedicated and segregated right of way for most of its route.

Other proposals may emerge in the next few years as the Government looks at alternative plans for mothballed Metro and Luas lines. The Railway Procurement Agency, which has been merged with the National Roads Authority into the National Transport Authority has been tasked with examining such proposals. It is therefore conceivable that Dublin may see another type of Tracks in the City in the future, but this time for guided buses.

CHAPTER 11
CONCLUSION

Beyond a shadow of doubt, years of neglect and low investment in the capital's rail system created many problems for the travelling public. Public perception of the services in place was also poor for a considerable period. Government after government seemed to favour road transport and in particular the private car over not only rail transport, but public transport in general. When new suburbs were planned, developed and allowed to sprawl, the authorities allowed such development based upon an already inadequate road network that had been planned years before. The warnings of expert transport consultants such as AM Voorhees that the road network would be inadequate to handle traffic by the 1980s were studiously ignored, and the sprawl was allowed to continue unchecked. This situation was made worse by alleged corruption in the planning system in Dublin, where, it was claimed, areas could be rezoned for development if the right people were paid off. The result was a city crippled with traffic as the economy started to grow. The threat was that economic expansion could really be hindered by poor infrastructure, and most importantly, Dublin commuters' patience was almost at breaking point. Something had to be done. Dublin was choking itself to death. Finally, in the 1990s the 'Powers That Be' started to recognise that investment in rail-based transport in the capital was urgently required.

As a last word, if and when Metro North eventually reaches the airport, it will not be able to claim the honour of getting the first rail vehicle to the site. Iarnród Éireann actually has that honour already and it was achieved in a very unique way. In 1994, when the first locomotive of the EMD 201 class arrived in the country from Canada, it was flown in on a giant Antanov aircraft. *(Iarnród Éireann)*

It is of course one of life's ironies that Ireland's economic slowdown, which later became an economic disaster, has occurred just as further plans for expansion of the railway network, Metro and Luas were planned. Many important projects have been long-fingered, and possibly some may never happen. Metro North had been well advanced in terms of design and planning and construction contracts were on the point of being let out when the project was suspended indefinitely. The DART underground interconnector wasn't far behind when it too ground to a halt. Metro West and the Lucan Luas, to be finished mid-way through the second decade of this century, will not now happen until who knows when. Strangely, a plan proposed almost 20 years ago but that didn't figure in any of the proposed projects of the last decade, may actually come to fruition, and that is an extension of the DART from Clongriffin, near Howth Junction, to the Airport (in lieu of Metro North).

Just like the old days, road projects seem to be getting priority and the strong economic case for going ahead with well advanced rail projects is being ignored. Such rail projects could help stimulate the economy, reduce unemployment and not only is this the right time to get value-for-money construction, but the long term benefits of having the infrastructure in place when the economy recovers are clear for anyone with even a basic grasp of economics.

There is of course, no doubt that Dublin is in a better place from a public transport point of view these days, thanks to the improvements and expansion of the last two decades. One can only hope that political commonsense will return, and that the successes will be built upon, so that one day Dublin will have a truly comprehensive and integrated rail-based public transport network.

Railway workers maintaining the line outside Kingsbridge (later Heuston) in the 1950s. *(Iarnród Éireann)*

OTHER BOOKS BY DÓNAL MURRAY

Irish Language
(all published by Coiscéím)

Airm Ollscriosta
Rianta na Cathrach
An Tarrtháil
Scéal na nUachtarán
Ar an Traein ó Thuaidh
Greim an Fhir Bháite

English
(Published by Midland Publishing and Ian Allan)

Rails around Dublin
Great Southern Railways

(Self published)

Weapons of Mass Destruction (novel)
Light Rail Infrastructure
Bus Rapid Transit for the 21st Century

For more information on this author visit:
www.donalmurray.co

Probably one of my first railway photographs ever was this one taken at Bray station in September 1978 at the tender age of seven. The occasion was an RPSI steam excursion behind number ex-GSWR 0-6-0 No 186. Although I was most impressed by the then nearly 100 year old steam locomotive, I was more interested in photographing the CIÉ 201 (C) class on a suburban service. At the time it was nothing out of the ordinary, but so much about this photograph is now history. The 201 class were withdrawn from service more than a quarter of a century ago and electric suburban trains in the form of the DART have been serving Bray station since 1984. It would also be unthinkable these days to have children sitting on the edge of a railway footbridge, particularly when there is now live overhead line equipment below! *(Dónal Murray)*